LAHORE
Places, People, Stories

LAHORE
Places, People, Stories

Aamir Butt

All rights reserved for the Author

Book:	Lahore (Places, People, Stories)
Author:	Aamir Butt
Publishing Year: 2024
Quantity:	500
Price:	2000

Dedication

Dedicated to
my mother,
Tanvir Butt,
all the Relatives and Friends in Lahore
whose existence is the reason, I love to visit this city.

چند کلیاں نشاط کی چن کر مدتوں محو یاس رہتا ہوں
تیرا ملنا خوشی کی بات سہی تجھ سے مل کر اداس رہتا ہوں

After gathering a few moments of happiness, I remain in sorrow for ages,

Meeting you is a reason for joy, I become sad when I meet you,

-Sahir Ludihanvi

When I have fears that I may cease to be
   Before my pen has gleaned my teeming brain,
Before high-pilèd books, in charactery,
   Hold like rich garners the full ripened grain;
When I behold, upon the night's starred face,
   Huge cloudy symbols of a high romance,
And think that I may never live to trace
   Their shadows with the magic hand of chance;
And when I feel, fair creature of an hour,
   That I shall never look upon thee more,
Never have relish in the faery power
   Of unreflecting love—then on the shore
Of the wide world I stand alone, and think
Till love and fame to nothingness do sink.

- John Keats

Contents

1	Introduction	11
2	Lahore	17
3	Where is my home	19
4	Lahories	23
5	Lhore Lhore aye (Lahore is Lahore)	25
6	The French mercenary and the girl from Lahore	31
7	And Lahore was never the same again	35
8	Ravi	39
9	On the grave of Bamba Sutherland	43
10	Red Sufi of Lahore	45
11	Mian Mir	51
12	Pen is mightier than the sword	55
13	He who has not seen Wazir Khan Mosque has not seen Lahore	59
14	Sir Ganga Ram	63
15	The riddle of Malik Ayaz	67
16	The Gun	69

17	Amrita and Sahir: A love story from Lahore	73
18	Progressive Writers Association	81
19	Lahore Fort	87
20	Maharaja Ranjit Singh	91
21	The Lion and the Peacock	101
22	Rustam-e-Insanyat (Champion of Humanity)	103
23	Bradlaugh Hall	105
24	Manto and Lahore	109
25	Unsung Hero	121
26	One of Lahore's greatest sons	125
27	Raqs Zanjeer Pahen ker bhe kya jata hai (One can dance in Chains as well!)	133
28	To die a dog's death (kuttay key maut merna)	137
29	Chandni Ratain (Moonlit Nights)	141
30	Making Movies in Lahore	143
31	Payar keya tu derna kya	149
32	Anarkali Fact or Fiction	155
33	Jews of Lahore	163
34	The Legend of Dulla Bhatti	167
35	The Other Amrita	169
36	Kabhi Kabhi	173
37	First Pakistani National Anthem and a poet from Lahore	177
38	Breakfast at Faletti's	183
39	The real Bhagat Singh	187

40	Durgha Devi, a freedom fighter from Lahore	193
41	Tombs of Jehangir and Noor Jehan	197
42	For the love of a Horse	201
43	Mohammad Rafi	205
44	Heera Mandi and Payasa	209
45	Koh a Noor (Mountain of Light) in Lahore	213
46	Hum Jo Tareek Rahon Mein Maray Gaye	219
47	Smash All the Mirrors	223
48	Bahar Lahori!	229
49	A Meeting in Lahore	233
50	Ghazi Ilam Din and Jinnah at Lahore High Court	239
51	Lala Amarnath, the swashbuckler from Lahore	243
52	From Russia with love to Lahore	249
53	Amrita and Lahore	253
54	When Tagore called	259
55	Khawja Khurshid Anwar, the melodist from Lahore	265
56	Kipling's Lahore	271
57	Javeed Manzil	275
58	Epilogue	279

Introduction

In the end, all lives are just stories, and most are soon forgotten.

We do not live once; we live every day, but we die twice: once physically and the second time when there is no one left to remember us and our stories.

We can change everything except for our parents and the place where we were born. I was born in Lahore, and although I have lived in many places and even now do not live in Lahore, it remains one of the two places I consider my home.

I was born in Lahore more than half a century ago, but never actually lived there. My father was always getting posted here and there, and by the time I could form memories, he had been posted out of Lahore. My earliest memories are from Abbottabad. However, Lahore always was a part of my life. My youngest paternal aunt, who lived with us until she got married, moved to Lahore as my new uncle was permanently based there, and so my memories of the 1960s are of frequent trips to Lahore to spend a few days in her house. I used to look forward to these trips as, besides other things, the first TV station had been installed in Lahore, and I loved watching TV programs like Alif-Noon, etc.

The trips to Lahore were interrupted for a while when my father got posted to Karachi in the late '60s. In 1973, he was posted again, this time to Rawalpindi, and we drove by car there, stopping over in Lahore.

For the next 20 years, Rawalpindi/Islamabad remained my home. Even though my father was posted to various locations during this time, to provide educational stability, I stayed in that area, finishing my medical school and starting my job at a hospital. During these years, there were several trips to Lahore every year of various durations, every visit a source of joy and entertainment. These interludes include my marriage, which took place in Lahore as my in-laws are paka-Lahories,(native Lahories) and the birth of my first child, which also took place in Lahore.

In 1992, I moved to the UK and have lived there ever since. My parents had settled in Islamabad after my father's retirement, but soon after my father passed away in 1996, my mother moved to Lahore, where most of her family lived.

Since then, I have visited Lahore every year. As the years have gone by, I have started to discover Lahore like I never did in the past. I have developed an interest in the historical heritage of this city, visiting places of interest after learning the history behind them. And as time goes by, the urge inside me to learn and discover more keeps increasing. Fortunately, social media has allowed me to become friends with other Lahoris with similar interests.

People might say, "How come I can claim to be in love with Lahore considering I have never actually been a resident of this city?" Well, I don't think one needs to live in a place to love it. The writer Anna Suvorova, who was the most knowledgeable person on Lahore history I know of, was not only from Lahore but not even Punjabi or Pakistani!

The visits to Lahore are not without some trepidation. Over the years, religious intolerance and violence have increased, or at least the awareness of it has. People like me are therefore apprehensive, as the same social media which helps us find like-minded people also exposes us to those who may not like how we think. Still, each time I set off for Lahore, I am looking forward to another period of relaxation interwoven with adventures to discover more parts of this ancient city.

No one who belongs to the Indian Subcontinent can deny the iconic status of the city of Lahore. Along with Calcutta and to a lesser extent (in my opinion) Delhi, and, Bombay: Lahore has a unique character, and people from Lahore carry it within their hearts no matter where in the world they live.

Over the years, I have written many notes and essays that are connected to Lahore in some way. For some, the connection to Lahore is obvious as a write-up on a Lahore landmark or place I visited; for others, the connection is a bit more subtle. This book is a collection of these pieces and in a way, is my homage to the city of Lahore, which I have carried with me wherever I have travelled.

This collection of pieces written over the last 10 years is bit like a ghazal, with each item independent of others yet loosely connected to the theme of love and the love of Lahore is the bond that holds it together. I hope these pieces on multiple topics will illustrate the reason why this city holds such fascination to me, although personal feelings cannot ever be fully explained to others.

Many of the stories will tell you how, before partition, people from various parts of India and even from other parts of the world decided to move to Lahore. While the attraction may have been due to the fact that, Lahore had some of the best educational institutions and might have offered better economic opportunities, what needs to be highlighted is that one of the main reasons for such decisions was that Lahore was one of the most, in fact probably the most, tolerant city in India and perhaps in the world. The people of Lahore accepted everyone who became a Lahori with open arms and made little or no distinction based on colour, caste, or religion.

No wonder the most tolerant of Mughal emperors, Akbar, moved his capital to Lahore, for his egalitarian ideas were most welcome here. Another of the many examples of the inclusive nature of Lahori culture is that when cricket started to become popular in India under British patronage, unlike in cities like Bombay and Karachi where teams were composed along communal lines, in Lahore it was between clubs and colleges which had players of different religions playing in the same team. For example, Lala Amarnath, the future captain of India, was a star player for the Crescent Club of Lahore.

It is one of the greatest tragedies of history that the tolerant, inclusive Lahore is no longer there. Religious intolerance and economic stagnation means that people from other parts of the world no longer have the desire to move to Lahore, and many who live in Lahore are looking for a chance to move abroad.

For the information contained in the articles, I am thankful to the writers/researchers Anna Suvorova, Abdul Majid Sheikh, Tahir Kamran, and Wikipedia, as well as many personal friends who have helped me to discover Lahore and its various aspects.

These include Ishtiaq Ahmed, Tahir Malik, Shahid Malik,

Irfan Anwar, Saeed Ahmed, Omar Khan, Osman Khan, Saima Khan, Mansoor Azam, Huma Price, Farjad Nabi, Huma Omar, Naveed Handerson, Nada Hasan, Meral Murat Khan, Muhammad Atiq, Waheed uz Zaman, Nadim Butt, Shahbaz Ali, Mansour Irfani, Tajamul Hasan, Dr Mubarak Mehdi, Wasim Altaf, Arshad Mahmood, Naheed Omar, Mansour Shah. I am sure there are others I have forgotten, for which I apologize.

I am thankful to my wife Maryam and daughters Zoha, Aanya and Nadine who helped with the cover of the book and encouraged me to publish it when I had doubts.

Special thanks to my uncle Soroush Irfani who helped a novice like me with publishing of a book.

And finally, I am thankful to Mohammad Fahad and AKS publications, who published and promoted this book with great efficiency and enthusiasm.

Lahore

"I'm tracing words on her bare shoulders.
I make an L, and she asks
"Isn't it too early to write Love"
I silently continue to write "Lahore"
I draw
It's empty 2 a.m. roads
A car going on the left lane
On the canal road
"kiya Yehi pyaar hai?" of Kishore
Playing on the radio.
The moon is reflecting in the muddy
Canal water.
The canal running through Lahore
Like her hair divide her back in two-unequal parts.
My lover, Lahore- the goddess of inequality.
Pashmeena shawls delicately resting on waxed bare arms,
Keeping them warm, around the bonfire.
The starving kid on the footpath
Selling boiled eggs.
His little hands freezing cold

as over-boiled eggs.
My Lahore- smitten by revolutionary poems of Faiz
Recited over a glass of whiskey,
Serenading the beautiful women,
Whom fathers, husbands, sons run the system.
The Nizam, which Jalib rejected.
His words equally radical never made it to warm rooms.
He kept on shivering in cold,
Like the egg seller.
My Lahore, would you remember me
The way you remember the Aurangzeb- Majestic Badshahi Mosque
Or would you forget me like your beloved prince- Dara Shikoh,
Killed and forgotten.
My lover is waiting for me to return
But my mind keeps on going to your memory
You, my treacherous mistress,
Who might have already forgotten me."

(Jasir Shahbaz)

Where is my home?

Where is my home?

Written after one of my visits to Lahore.

Waking up this morning, for a few moments, I was not sure if I am in Lahore or Ferriby! However, it soon dawned on me that I was in the house which is now the one I have lived in for the longest period of my life and the bed I have most slept in. I have lived roughly half of my life in England and half in Pakistan, but this house is the single most lived-in house for me.

People like me, first-generation immigrants, spend their lives never sure which place they should call home. For all practical purposes, home is the country where we have a house, where we make a living, where we pay taxes, and most importantly, where our children live. However, we are not like our children who were born in our new country. We spent our childhood, growing up years, and part of adult life in another country, and while that country still exists, and we visit her, this sense of not being entirely sure where we belong remains.

I had rather a nomadic life, when I used to live in Pakistan, in the sense that instead of staying permanently in Lahore, the city I was born in, I moved every few years to different cities before settling down in Rawalpindi when I was 18. It was from here that I moved to England in my thirties.

Although, until I moved to UK, Pakistan was my home, I was not 100% sure in which part of that country was that home! Earlier, when I used to come temporarily to the UK for exams etc., I missed the Rawalpindi-Islamabad area as it was there in those days where my parents and friends were living. When in those days in England, revising for exams, I used to sit and listen to Faiz Sahib's poetry, and these lines came up:

دیار غیر میں محرم اگر نہیں کوئی
تو فیضؔ ذکرِ وطن اپنے روبرو ہی سہی

'In the foreign land, if you cannot find a friend, then Faiz talks about your homeland with yourself.'

It would be Rawalpindi-Islamabad that would conjure up in my brain.

Today, after I have settled in the UK, my mother has moved to Lahore, and it is Lahore I spend 99% of my time while visiting Pakistan, I think of Lahore as my home in Pakistan. Strange as it sounds, I became a Lahori after I migrated to the UK!

The difference between humans and Artificial Intelligence remains the presence or absence of emotions. Emotions we have are attached to other humans, not as it is projected in popular slogans the land itself. We often hear about the bones of ancestors and the fragrance of the native soil. Personally, I feel no shame in declaring that I feel nothing for such dead things. I don't feel any love for stones and bricks and other non-living items in Pakistan or

England. I am sure someone will be thinking, "So you don't care about your dead father?" Well, yes, but all my attachments to my father are from the times when he was alive. I have no love for the plot of land where he is buried because he is not there. He is in my heart, his memories are in my brain, and those are the real things, not bones and dust. The memories are what I can carry with me wherever I go.

Our attachment to our land of birth is due to our relationships, the memories of the good times we have spent there, and the love we received and still do, if we are fortunate enough when we visit. The love and longing I have for Pakistan is due to the people whom I love who live there. My mother, my relatives, and my friends are the reasons for my love, not the dust and bones.

I think we have to conclude that first-generation immigrants like me have two homes, one in the country we were born in and the second where we have moved to. This reminds me of lines from Neil Diamond's song,

'Well I'm New York City born and raised,
but nowadays
I'm lost between two shores.
L.A.'s fine, but it ain't home,
New York's home, but it ain't mine no more.'

Well, life goes on as long as I am alive and retain cognition, there will be other trips to Lahore and Pakistan.

چند کلیاں نشاط کی چن کر مدتوں محو یاس رہتا ہوں

تیرا ملنا خوشی کی بات سہی تجھ سے مل کر اداس رہتا ہوں

chand kaliyāñ nashāt kī chun kar muddatoñ mahv-e-yās rahtā huuñ

terā milnā k͟hushī kī baat sahī tujh se mil kar udaas rahtā huuñ

"After gathering a few moments of happiness, I remain

lost in grief for a long time,
   Meeting you is a moment of happiness; I don't know why I become sad."

(Sahir Ludihanvi)

Lahories

Whenever I tell people I am going to Lahore, they ask me if it is safe. For sure, their concern is in the context of terrorism, suicide bombings, law and order, etc. However, I have never felt unsafe in this way, but I must warn those who are thinking of visiting and have a faint heart that Lahore traffic can be scary. It looks as if there are no traffic laws or if there are, no one cares about them. Every car, rickshaw, and motorcycle driver seems to have left his house with, *sir pay kaffan bandh ker-* a death wish.Approaching a roundabout is a sight to behold as everyone thinks they have the right of way and drives without care. No one ever gives way, and merging in is a case of playing chicken.

Everyone looks to be in a hurry to get somewhere; one wonders why, as no one arrives at the time they said they would. So, if they tell you they will visit you at 7, they come at 8, and that is when they do you a favour. The other day I went to a meeting which was to start at 6:30 and started at 7:30 as the speakers did not arrive till then. Once my mother was invited to a wedding reception; the invite asked to come at 6 PM. Knowing the trend, she went at 7 PM and no one was there. When she phoned the hosts, they said they would be along by 10!

An anecdote I read by a foreign visitor to Lahore may help explain this anomaly. The visitor narrates how he noticed the Lahoris risking life and limb to get somewhere. When the traffic had to stop as a gate on a railway crossing was closed, a man on a bicycle got off, put the bike on his shoulder, climbed over the gate, and ran across the track while the train approached. The visitor was impressed thinking that the man must be hurrying to an appointment and did not want to be late, so diligent he was that he even put his life at risk. However, he was shocked when the gate opened and after travelling a short distance, he found the same man leaning against his bike and watching a monkey show by the roadside!

By and large, the life of Lahoris revolves around food. Even in times of severe economic hardship, the restaurants and eateries are always packed, and Lahoris can be seen devouring large meals with gusto.

The other specialty of Lahories is *jugat bazi*. In English, this can best be described as a humorous satirical comment targeting a hapless friend or stranger. Although to someone not tuned in to the Lahori sense of humour, this exchange can look insulting; it is done good-naturedly, and the victim, if Lahori, does not take offense, only waits for his turn to take revenge.

Lhore Lhore aye (Lahore is Lahore)

Like the saying about Rome, "All roads lead to Rome," there is one about Lahore, *"Janay Lahore nehien wakhaya o jammaya he nien* (The one who has not seen Lahore has not been born)."

Not many cities of the world have such catchphrases associated with them. I can't think of another city in the Subcontinent with such a distinction, though I may be wrong.

Without doubt, the city of Lahore has held a special significance in the history of this region and continues to hold a prominent place in the hearts of those who have been linked to it in some way. Lahore is called the heart of Pakistan, but its splendour long predates Pakistan.

In former times, Lahore was compared with Isfahan, the magnificent capital of the Safavid Persian empire. The Lahoris, of course, thought that it is the other way around! There is a famous Farsi saying that goes, *"Ispahan Nesf-i Jehan ast'* (Isfahan is half the world), and Lahoris used to counter it with *"agar Lahore nabud Isphehan nesf-jehan bud"* (If there was no Lahore then Isfahan would be half the world). In fact, according to their estimation, Isfahan and

Shiraz together equalled half of Lahore!

Such confidence is not totally misplaced, for Lahore has not failed to impress unbiased observers. For example, John Milton in his famous epic poem Paradise Lost (1667) describes what Adam sees when he looks at the earth from Paradise:

> *'His eye might there command wherever stood*
> *City of old or modern fame, the seat*
> *Of mightiest empire, from the destined walls*
> *Of Cambalu, seat of Cathain Caobserversn,*
> *And Samarchand by Oxus, Temir's throne,*
> *To Pacquin, of Sinaen kings, and thence*
> *To Agra and Lahor of Great Mogul.....'*

Like all ancient cities, the exact origin of Lahore is shrouded in mystery and coloured by mythology. According to mythology, Lahore's founder was one of the sons of Ram named Lava or Loh (his twin Kassu is responsible for nearby Kasur), and its ancient name was either Lava-kot or Loh-Kot. The word "Kot" comes from the Rajput language and means fortress or stronghold, so it seems that Lahore's real founders were Rajputs. Many historians think they were from the Bhatti clan of Rajputs.

The date this city was created is unknown, and although some claim it was mentioned in the 7th Century BC Ramayana as Loh-Pur, the more authentic first mention in historical records is from the book on Geography by Claudius Ptolemy (90-168 AD), who calls it Labokla. So, we can deduce that it is at least 2000 years old, which does not make it one of the oldest cities in the world but still quite mature historically. Here, I would mention a paper I read by Khwaja Abdul Rashid Sahib, where he claims that Lahore is one of the only 3 eternal cities of the world that have continuously existed for 10,000 years, so some scholars consider it to be much older than when it was first mentioned in written records.

The first time this city has been mentioned as Lahore is in the book Jamir al-Tawarikh by Rashid ud Din of Hamadan. This book was written around 1316. However, that does not mean it was called by this name from there on; various variations of the name continued to be used side by side until Lahore became the only one at some unknown stage in time.

The astronomer/physician Al-Biruni wrote a book on India in which he mentions Lahore by the name Lohawar, while Data Gunj Bakhsh, who is Lahore's patron saint and who was buried there in 1076, calls it Lahawur. Please note that "awar" or "awur" both originate from Sanskrit "awarana," which means a fort or a stronghold and thus is synonymous with "kot." There are other cities in Pakistan which end in Kot (Sialkot) or awar (Peshawar). Eventually, the present name Lahore evolved from this.

The first detailed description of Lahore is found in a Persian book by an unknown author called Hudud al-Alam (regions of the world), which appears to have been written around 982 AD. In this, Lahore is described as a city of impressive temples, large markets, and huge orchards. It also mentions the mud wall (called Kucha Kot by Rajputs) which surrounded what is now the old Lahore walled city.

In 1002, Lahore became part of the Ghaznavid empire, and by 1012, it became the capital of this empire. One of Iqbal's verses is:

Aik he saff mei-n kharay ho gaye Mahmud o Ayaz
Na koi banda raha aur na koi banda nawaz

Mahmud and Ayaz stand shoulder to shoulder,
There was no master and there was no servant.
Mahmud of Ghazni was the king, and Ayaz was his

favourite slave, and verse of them standing at the same level during namaz (prayer congregation) is to illustrate Islamic egalitarianism. According to some accounts, after capturing Lahore, Mahmud made Ayaz its governor. At this time, the large-scale construction of Lahore fort started. Ayaz expanded the city by bringing in artisans from other parts of the empire and built a wall around the old city also. He died in Lahore and is buried in Rang Mahal *Mohalla*. When I visited his tomb, the caretaker declared that he was the first Pakistani governor of Punjab!

Lahore continued to attract conquerors who invaded India as they used to come from the North-West, and Lahore was in their way when marching towards Delhi and beyond.

In 1556, the greatest of the great Mughals, Akbar, became the emperor. His rule is distinguished by his great tolerance to followers of all religions, and it was appropriate that in 1586, he moved the capital of his empire to Lahore, the most tolerant of the cities not only in India but arguably the whole world.

Patras Bukhari, in his book *Lahore ka Jugraphia* (Geography of Lahore), tells us that of the routes that lead to Lahore, the two most famous are: One that comes from Peshawar and the other from Delhi. Central Asian invaders came by the Peshawar route, and invaders from the United Province via Delhi. The former are called the People of Sword and had names like Ghaznavi, Ghuri, etc. The latter were called the People of Speech, and they also skillfully used pseudonyms. Here Patras is referring to the many writers and poets who moved to Lahore from UP after 1947 and conquered it in their way. Unfortunately, a similar number or more of these also moved from Lahore to Delhi, Bombay, etc., a great loss for Lahore.

Today, despite its overflowing population, its fog and pollution, gas, water, and power shortages, Lahore continues to be the first love for the majority of Pakistani intelligentsia and common folk. It is the heart of Pakistan, and their hearts beat in rhythm with it.

As Faiz writes, declaring his everlasting love and longing for Lahore:

> *Sabza sabza sookh rahi hai pheeki zard do-perhar*
> *deewaron ko chat raha hai tanhai ka zehar*
> *duur ufaq tak ghati barthi uthi girti rehti hai*
> *kohar ki soorat be-robaq dardon ki gadli lehar*
> *basta hai is kohar ke peechay roshniyon ka shehar*
> *aye roshnioyon ke shehar, kaun kahey kis simt hai teri roshniyon ki rah*
> *har janib benoor khari hai hijr ki shehar panah*
> *thak key har so baith rahi hai shauq ki mand sipah*
> *aaj mera dil fikr mein hai aye roshniyon kay shehar*
> *shabkhoon se moonh pher na jaey armano ki ro*
> *khair ho teri lailaoon ki, in sab se keh do*
> *aaj ki shab jab diyay jalaein, oonchi rakhain lo!*

> *On each patch of green, from one shade to the next,*
> *the noon is erasing itself by wiping out all colour,*
> *becoming pale, desolation everywhere,*
> *the poison of exile painted on the walls.*
> *In the distance,*
> *there are terrible sorrows, like tides:*
> *they draw back, swell, become full, subside.*
> *They've turned the horizon to mist.*
> *And behind that mist is the city of lights,*
> *my city of many lights.*
> *How will I return to you, my city,*
> *where is the road to your lights? My hopes*

are in retreat, exhausted by these unlit, broken walls,
and my heart, their leader, is in terrible doubt.
But let all be well, my city, if under
cover of darkness, in a final attack,
my heart leads its reserves of longings
and storms you tonight. Just tell all your lovers
to turn the wicks of their lamps high
so that I may find you, Oh, city,
my city of many lights.
(Translation by Agha Shahid Ali)

The French mercenary and the girl from Lahore

Jean-François Allard was born in St. Tropez (now a famous playground for the rich and famous) in 1785. At a young age, he joined the army of Napoleon Bonaparte and distinguished himself for bravery, winning medals and promotions. When in 1815 Napoleon was defeated at Waterloo, Allard escaped from Europe and moved to Persia, then under Shah Abbas, where he joined his army. During his time there, he learned Persian.

In 1822, the British asked the Persian king to arrest all French officers in his service. Allard once again escaped and moving through Kabul in disguise, arrived in Lahore. Here he offered his service to Maharaja Ranjit Singh. In the next few years, he became Ranjit Singh's most trusted General, as he organized the elite fighting unit of the Khalsa Army, which was named *Fauj a Khas* (Special Forces). It was mainly because of the quality of the Sikh army under Ranjit Singh that the rapacious East India Company stayed out of Punjab during his lifetime, and for this, Ranjit Singh owed a lot to Allard. This is something he acknowledged by giving Allard a huge salary as well as many jagirs (fiefdoms) in Punjab.

Allard was a man for whom the army was his life. We do not know much about his earlier love life, although he had left a wife in France. This changed the day he saw Ranjit Singh's niece, the princess of Chamba, who is known as Banu Pan Dei. Allard was struck dumb by her beauty. Ranjit Singh, himself a great connoisseur of beautiful women, was able to see his friend's predicament and decided that he offered the hand of the beautiful princess. This was in 1826; Allard was 40, and the girl was said to be 13 or 14. However, who could refuse what Ranjit Singh decided? Was Banu forced into this marriage? Was Allard a paedophile? I am afraid these are questions we can only answer with our present-day values. As for what used to happen in those days, Allard and Banu were married.

No doubt Allard was smitten by his wife. The proof is that unlike his junior French general Ventura, also in Maharaja's service, who had a harem of 2,000 women, Allard remained a one-woman man, totally committed to Banu. Over the next 8 years, Allard and Banu had 5 children, one of them, a girl, died in infancy. They were buried in a tomb built in the vast garden of the villa they lived in.

In 1834, Allard asked Ranjit Singh to give him leave so that he could take his family to France and settle them there. "Why do you want to do this?" asked Ranjit, and Allard replied that he wants his children to have a good Catholic education, which is not possible in Lahore. Ranjit agreed but told him to come back. Allard promised he would come back soon. Allard then took his wife and 4 children along with their trusted maid to St. Tropez, where he built a palatial villa for them and settled them there. During the 2 years he lived with them, they had another child. Then, in 1836, Allard told Banu that he had to return to Punjab to fulfil his promise to Ranjit Singh but told her he would return to her as soon as possible. It seems he was expecting to come back once Ranjit Singh died.

What Banu did not know was that Allard, who was 27 years older, was afraid that if he died in Punjab and Banu was with him, she may be forced to commit Sati, and that is why he had brought her over to France. Apparently Allard had confused the practice of Satti and thought all Hindu women were supposed to perform it.

Allard returned to Punjab and continued to serve Ranjit Singh. He never saw Banu and his family again. In 1839, while on assignment in Peshawar, he died, most likely of a heart attack. His body was brought to Lahore, and he was buried with full military honours in a ceremony fit for a king between the graves of his two daughters (one other daughter from his French wife who had joined him in Lahore had died earlier).

The garden where these graves are is known in Lahore as *Kuri Bagh* (Daughter's Garden). Kuri means girl or daughter in Punjabi. Later on, most of the property was used to construct multi-story flats that were called Kuri Bagh Flats for a while before the name faded from the memory of Lahoris.

The graves of Allard and his Kuris (daughters) remained, and more recently, the French government initiated a project to repair and restore them, while at the same time, a statue of Ranjit Singh was constructed in St. Tropez.

It is now a very nice little mausoleum tucked away in a corner of old Lahore. Interestingly, its existence is not widely known, for when I went to visit it, even the shopkeeper a few yards away were unable to guide me to it.

As for Banu Pana Dei, even if she was a child bride of a

much older man, it looks like she did fall in love with him. Since he left, she would go to the pier every day expecting him to sail back to her. When in 1839, she was told he was dead and buried, she converted to Catholicism but refused to believe he was dead and continued to go to the pier every day to welcome him until her own death in 1884.

The palace Allard built for Banu in St. Tropez is now an upmarket boutique hotel. Once, I thought of staying there but gave up when the cheapest room was upwards of $1000 for a night.

And thus, this strange love story ended with a man born in St. Tropez buried in Lahore while the girl he loved, who was born in Lahore, is buried in St. Tropez!

And Lahore was never the same again

In 1955, MGM Studios decided to make a film based on a novel by John Masters called "The Bhowani Junction" (published in 1954). The story revolves around a young Anglo-Indian girl named Victoria Jones who works for the British army and is being courted by three suitors: a native Indian Sikh named Ranjit Kesal, a fellow Anglo-Indian called Patrick Taylor, and a British army officer, Colonel Rodney Savage. Set in pre-partition India with independence looming just over the horizon, much of the action takes place around railway tracks, as Victoria's father is in charge of a railway station. The exact location of this junction was unknown, but based on the description, it was thought to be Jhansi. Thus, the production team approached the Indian government to obtain permission to shoot the film there.

However, India, under Nehru's leadership, was vigorously following the line of non-alignment, and the Indian government viewed such a request by an American company with suspicion. After much deliberation, they decided that the project could proceed, provided the script was thoroughly scrutinized by Indian authorities (with a fee for that) and various tariffs and taxes were to be paid by

MGM to the Indian exchequer. Unhappy with these conditions, MGM turned to Pakistan, which readily approved the project with Lahore and its railway station as the location. Pakistani authorities even offered full cooperation from local police and military units, including the Lahore-based 1/13 Frontier Force Battalion, of which Colonel Savage was to be the commandant, rather than the 1/13 Gurkha battalion in the novel.

For the female lead, Victoria, MGM cast the actress, Ava Gardner. 33-year-old Ava was one of the top heroines of Hollywood at that time. In the bevy of blond actresses Ava stood out with her raven hair and thus was more suited to play an Anglo-Indian. Ava's hair was not the only feature that separated her from other Hollywood beauties, for she was the archetypical wild child. For women, the tinsel town in those days was not as permissive as today, while the male leads were able to sow their wild oats the female actresses were supposed to be chaste and pure. Ava, however, did not care about such qualms, she lived her life as she pleased, drinking and smoking like the male icons and having love affairs like them.

Eva was then with her third husband, the legendary old blue eyes Frank Sinatra and the relationship was as rocky as it can be.

Just before Ava started working on "Bhowani Junction," her film "Barefoot Contessa" was released. In this film, she played the role of a nightclub dancer who captivates Humphrey Bogart when he sees her dancing barefoot, probably the only part of anatomy allowed to be bare in movies of those days. The film was a big hit in Lahore.

Upon her arrival, Ava received a red carpet-reception at the airport, and the national press gave her front-page coverage. The film stars were housed in Faletti's Hotel, then the best in the town, located near Mall Road, Lahore's equivalent of the Champs-Élysées during those times. While Mall Road is now congested with bumper-to-bumper traffic, Faletti's still has an Ava Gardner suite complete with a life-size portrait of the starlet.

During her over two-month stay in Lahore, Ava was often seen walking on Mall Road in the evenings, albeit with her shoes on due to the risk of tetanus and other risks. One memorable story recounted by writer Mustansar Tarrar involves four young boys, one of whom was possibly him, who were astonished to see Ava dressed in mid-thigh shorts, arm in arm with a gora, strolling on Mall Road. They followed her to a restaurant, where they managed to approach her and demand autographs. Ava obliged, signing their autograph books and even placing them against her thigh while the boy was still holding it, sending electric shocks up their spine. Each boy was convinced she was in love with him, and they all vowed, never to wash their hands.

Another anecdote involves a young man whose father ran an alcohol business in Lahore. At barely 18 years old, he was tasked with looking after esteemed guests during a party. Disappointed that Ava did not have anything bare while dressed in full-length trousers and shoes, he was astonished to see her match the male company in drinking and smoking. When the alcohol ran out, he rushed to get more, and when he escorted Ava to the toilet, he heard her shout on entering, 'God, this place smells f*****g s**t' to his utter disbelief.

Several locals had a role in the movie, mostly as extras. As the scene was set in India many of them had to wear Nehru caps during the shooting and although they did not like Pandit sahib at all they had no problems wearing his trademark cap as long as they got some dollars at the end of the day.

When the shooting was completed Ava Gardner left Lahore, and as Tarrar writes in his story, Lahore was never the same again.

As for who gets the girl in the end, while in the novel Victoria marries her fellow Anglo-Indian Patrick, the film alters this outcome. The native Indian suitor, Ranjit, is sidelined, while Patrick meets a heroic end, allowing Victoria to marry the dashing British Colonel and live happily ever after.

And what about Ava Gardner herself? Well, her real-life love story did not have a happy ending; real-life stories seldom do. Although Sinatra later confessed that she was the only true love of his life, they were unable to stay together. Partly because Sinatra thought that it was okay for him to chase other actresses while she should confine herself to his bed, and Ava thought it should be the other way around. They divorced in 1957. Ava went on in her merry way smoking, drinking, and having fun until her lungs gave up, and she died aged 67. Her last words were, 'I am so tired.'

Ravi

Jay Ravi wich pani koi nei
Tay apni kahani koi nei
If there is no water in Ravi
Then it is the end of our story

We are told by Sajjad Ali in his song 'Ravi'. While the song is written from the perspective of an expat walking by a river in another land and remembering his home where the river Ravi flows, there is no doubt that great cities are always connected to mighty rivers. There would be no London without the Thames and no Paris without the Seine. And for the city of Lahore, the river Ravi has always been the river associated with it.

One day, I decided to find out just how much water there is in the Ravi. I had read in an article by Majid Sheikh Sahib that when he went, a herd of buffaloes was struggling to take a bath. After an arduous journey through Lahore traffic, where it seems no motorbike has less than 4 and no car with less than 8 riders, I managed to reach the Ravi. Surprisingly, there was more water than I expected. There was enough water for the buffaloes, and there were even boats in the river. Still, no doubt, this is not a mighty flowing river but more of a stream or two, and although the water did not look too dirty from afar, I am told that most of what we see is industrial waste flowing into where once the Ravi flowed.

In ancient times, the Ravi used to flow by the walls of Lahore; indeed, before roads and railways, transportation of travelers and goods by the river was quicker and safer than by land, and most people visiting Lahore used to disembark at the ferry terminal at Khizri gate. This gate was so named because of the tale that Hazrat Khizar, who is in charge of the world's waterways, stepped out of the river and passed through this gate when he visited Lahore. In the 19th century, Maharaja Ranjit Singh is said to have positioned two caged lions on either side of the entrance as guards, and the name of the gate became Sheranwala Gate (Gate of Lions).

When in 1947, British India became independent as two different countries, the province of Punjab, so named because of 5 (actually there are 6) rivers flowing through it, was partitioned. And bewildered intellectuals like Manto wondered what else would be partitioned— for example, how would art be partitioned— the rivers were certainly partitioned, but not until 1960. And Ravi was given to India.

Since then, a significant change has taken place to the river; it now flows almost 5 miles further East than it used to and no longer passes near the walls of old Lahore. And of course, the amount of water that flows through it is usually just a trickle except in the flood season. It is said that when the Indian dams under construction are completed in 2022, there will be no water in the river at all.

There is an old saying that whenever in history the city of Lahore has risen, Ravi has been at its centre, and there may be some truth in this, so the prophecy of Ravi's imminent demise is distressing for anyone from Lahore.

Still, there is some hope, as a long-talked-about plan calls for creating an artificial lake in the place of Ravi and making it the centre of a planned rather than haphazard expansion of the city.

And by listening to the words of a song by Jimmy Nail about another once mighty river (Tyne in this case), we can keep our hopes alive:

> *This was a big river*
> *I want you all to know that I was proud*
> *This was a big river, but that was long ago,*
> *That's not now*
> *This is a big river,*
> *And in my heart I know it will rise again*
> *The river will rise again*

On the grave of Bamba Sutherland

In a quiet corner of Gora Qabristan of Lahore (The Christian Graveyard), lies the grave of Princess Bamba Sutherland, the last descendant of Maharaja Ranjit Singh, the first ruler of Punjab who was from Punjab.

After being forced to sign over the empire his father created to the British, Dalip Singh was exiled to London at the age of 16. There, Queen Victoria took him under her wing and tried to get him married to a girl from a British aristocratic family. Almost certainly to spite her and show defiance, he married Bamba Muller, a girl born out of wedlock to a German father and Ethiopian mother. From this union, there were 6 children, 2 sons, and 4 daughters. Bamba Singh was the eldest daughter born in 1869.

After her father died in 1893, she developed a desire to visit Lahore but was refused permission repeatedly by the British authorities till 1912. After that first visit, she visited several times more, and in 1915 she married Doctor David Sutherland, a physician who was the principal of Lahore's prestigious King Edwards Medical College, and settled in Lahore for good. She befriended many Indian revolutionaries like Lala Lajpat Rai and was also a friend of

Allama Iqbal. When Dr. Sutherland retired in 1926, he moved back to Scotland, but Bamba decided to stay in her beloved Lahore.

She knew that both her grandmother Rani Jindan Kaur (died 1863) and father the deposed Maharaja Duleep Singh (died 1893) had no greater desire than a chance to come back to Lahore, a wish the British refused to allow even after their deaths. After much effort, she succeeded in getting Rani Jindan's remains shifted to Lahore, but her desire to get her father's body relocated to Ranjit Singh's Samadhi was not fulfilled. Bamba Sutherland outlived all her siblings as well as the two children her father had from his second marriage. She died in 1957, and as per her instructions, a Persian couplet by Saadi was inscribed on her tombstone which translates as: "The difference between a king and a commoner disappears as soon as one meets his destined end. If you dig up the dust of the dead, you will not be able to tell if he was rich or a beggar."

Strangely, neither she nor any of the other children fathered by Dalip Singh had any children of their own. The reason for this remains a mystery.

Red Sufi of Lahore

Lahore is a city of Sufi (Mystic) shrines; it is said to have more than 100 of these. The most popular is that of Data Ganj Bakhsh; this is the one that receives the most visitors. Also, Pakistani politicians and generals including Zia, Bhutto, Sharifs, etc., have patronized Data Darbar. Although the Deobandi version of Islam that was favoured by Zia ul Haq drew its inspiration from Wahabi/Salafi doctrine originating in Arabia and which opposes all shrines considering them to be shirk (a type of sin), in Pakistan, there has always been a strong presence of Barelvi Islam which is more indigenous to the Indian Subcontinent and places great emphasis on Sufi Mystics and their shrines. This tradition was established during the days of the Delhi Sultanate (12th Century) when the Muslim Sultans ruled under the spiritual blessing of Sheikhs. These Sheikhs were mostly immigrants from Iran and Iraq, and once they became established in one city patronized by the ruler, their children continued their preaching after them. Some of their practices were not consistent with orthodox Islam; often poetry and music played an important role at their khanqahs. Amir Khusro invented the Qawali form of rendition and even added new musical instruments to praise his spiritual guide Sheikh Nizamuddin Auliya of Delhi.

However, Ali Hajweri (Ganj Bakhsh) was a more traditionalist follower of Islam emphasizing the importance of sharia, so he was promoted more and has become the favoured mystic saint of Lahore. Ali Hajweri is also considered to be responsible for the spread of Islam in India and thus, despite that he was a Persian scholar from Ghazni who migrated to Lahore, he has become far more popular than indigenous Sufis of Lahore. This has been seen in the last 100 years as a more Islamic identity has been formed or forced among the people of Lahore. Out of the 3 major sufis who are buried in Lahore, Hajwari, Mian Mir, and Madho Lal, the last was the only one born in Lahore and is the most colorful and controversial.

His shrine is located in the Baghbanpura part of Lahore. To get there, one needs to pass through narrow congested streets, so a skilled driver is needed. And make sure if you ask for directions, you do not say Madhu Lal ka *Mazar* (shrine) but ask for his *Darbar* (court) for he is considered a *Zinda Pir* (living mystic) and listens to you when you talk to him!

The shrine is quite spacious with the entrance painted red. Some who do not know about this mystic may be baffled by finding 2 instead of one grave inside. The fact is that Madho Lal Hussain is not one but two people. I will explain this a bit later.

First let me explain the significance of red. Red is the colour of blood; it also symbolizes new birth or something new and different. In this context, it is a colour of revolution, of a break with tradition and with what society considers as the norm. Among the Sufis, red is also the colour favoured by those who break away from the more traditional practice of religion, even Sufism. While Sufis favour white or green colours, those who indulge in unconventional practices often wear red clothes and are called Lal (red). This reminds me that the term Surkhay (reds) is often used in a derogatory way by the Pakistani traditionalists towards those with socialist ideas.

This is now the only shrine in Lahore where *Dhamal*, the popular mystic dance, is still performed, but the caretaker was a bit elusive when I asked him about this. The thing is this dancing is severely condemned by the fundamentalists who consider it un-Islamic and vulgar. A few years ago, a suicide attack during *Dhamal*,at the tomb of another red Sufi Shahbaz Qalandar in Sindh killed more than 80 men and women doing the *Dhamal*,performance.

The Sufi buried in this shrine was named Shah Husain. He was born in 1538 and became a leading Muslim scholar and cleric. Then when he was 36, his world changed. It is said this happened when he was reciting the Quran and came to a verse which said, "The world is just games and plays," and he said if it is so then that is how I will live my life. So, he trimmed his beard, let his hair grow wild, and spent his time dancing, singing, and drinking (a bit like the story of Rumi) instead of praying and preaching. He also started composing poetry with the names of Fakir *Nemaina* (the lowest of beggars) and Faqir *Julaha (*weaver which was his family occupation before converting to Islam). Shah Husain also invented the *Kafi* form of Punjabi poetry which consists of short poems of 6 to 10 lines aimed to be sung and are often used in *Qawalis*.

The most controversial part of this story is that Shah Hussain fell madly in love with a Hindu Brahman boy called Madhu. His love was reciprocated, and Madho started spending time with him. According to the official story,

Madhu's family after initial objection was convinced by Shah Hussain's spiritual powers and all converted to Islam. I feel this is just made up to make this tale kosher; it is more likely that both Shah Hussain and Madho left their respective religions and lived together in defiance of all religious and conventional norms of morality and society.

Madho outlived Shah Hussain by 48 years and is buried next to him; his grave is in a different colour to Shah Hussain's, which is in red. Their tombstones retain their individual identities with the fused name Madhu Lal Hussain displayed on the wall.

Shah Husain is an example of a *Malamati* Sufi, those who intentionally degrade themselves so that society condemns and abuses them.

In one of his kafis he says
Vay Madho! Main wadda theyaa badnaam!
Raati pi ke dukh da piyaala tureyaa suwairon shaam!
Ki aakhaan main ki si peeti? Loki dassan haraam!
Kaafar aakhan saarey mainoon laawan sabh ilzaam!
Mukh fairan sub maidey wallon naal karraan dushnaam!
Rowey Hussain maidey Saain nu Madho chheti peej salaam!

O Madho! I have been greatly defamed!
After drinking last night from my cup of sorrows, I have wandered from morning till night
What can I say that I had drunk? People say it was the forbidden wine!
All here call me an infidel and accuse me of

transgression!

They turn back their faces from me and abuse me!

Wails Hussain, O Madho quick, send my greeting to my Master!

Also associated with Madho Lal Husain and his shrine is the *Mela Chiraghan* (festival of lamps) of Lahore. This used to be the biggest festival of the city, and in the 19th century, Maharaja Ranjit Singh, who was a great admirer of Madho Lal, no doubt recognizing him as a fellow Punjabi, would personally lead the procession from his palace in the Red Fort to the Shrine of Madho Lal barefoot and holding a lighted lamp in his hand. He was accompanied by thousands of Muslims, Sikhs, and Hindus.

It looks like all Sufi shrines forbid women from approaching the grave. In this shrine, the notice did not just say women are not allowed but added the word "strictly," and I guess with this Sufi being the one most openly displaying his unconventional sexuality, this looks ironically acceptable!

Mian Mir

Visiting shrines of holy men is very popular among Muslims in the Subcontinent. Lahore is said to have more than 150 such shrines. Out of these, two are considered as the patron saints of Lahore: Data Ganj Bakhsh and Mian Mir. Data Sahib is more popular, and his *Mazar* is visited by a lot more people; however, Mian Mir is more illustrious among the two in my opinion.

This saint was born in Persia and arrived in Lahore via Sind around 1575. He lived here until his death in 1638 at the ripe old age of 88. His piety and wisdom were admired far and wide, and both the Mughal emperors who reigned during his time, Jehangir and Shah Jehan, were big fans and visited him many times.

Legend says that when Jehangir came to visit him, he was stopped at the gate and had to wait before he was called in. When he remarked sarcastically as to why a faqir (ascetic) needs door guards, Mian Mir immediately replied, "They are there to keep out dogs and greedy men." Jehangir then asked Mian Mir to pray for success in the forthcoming Deccan campaign. At this moment, another devotee arrived and offered a gift of one Rupee to Mian Mir, who asked him to give it to some poor man outside. The man said he had tried but no one wants it. Mian Mir then pointed towards Jehangir and said, "Give it to him, he is the poorest man here, for despite such a vast kingdom, he wants more."

Mian Mir is best known for his close friendship with the 5th Sikh guru Arjun Sahib. When Guru Arjun decided to construct the famous Golden Temple in Amritsar, he requested Mian Mir to come and lay the foundation stone for it. There could not have been any greater respect given to anyone by the Sikh guru. Note, some sources dispute this story.

Mian Mir was also the spiritual guide of the favourite Mughal prince Dara Shikoh during the rule of Shah Jehan. After he passed away, Dara Shikoh started the construction of a magnificent tomb made of marble and red sandstone. However, when only the base of the tomb had been built, Dara Shikoh was killed by his brother Aurangzeb, who confiscated all the marble and sandstone and used it to build the massive Badshahi Mosque.

So, the rest of the tomb was made of cheap bricks and painted over. Unlike many other Mughal buildings, the tomb is very original, for the Sikhs did not damage it as there was no marble or expensive material to take away.

Dara Shikoh was the favourite of Emperor Shah Jehan. He was a mystic-poet who was close to the teachings of Sufi-saints like Mian Mir. These teachings did not preach a dogmatic exclusive Islam but a religion that promoted inter-faith harmony and inclusiveness of other faiths. Shikoh was also the governor of Lahore and much loved by the people. His defeat in the power struggle was a blow to the city as well as the syncretic religion teachers like Mian Mir promoted.

Today at the door, a sign says that women are not

allowed to enter. I have seen this at all Sufi shrines that women are not allowed to enter the chamber where the grave is or go near it. I once asked the caretaker why this was so, and he gave the most hilarious explanation: apparently, the Sufis are not dead but sleeping. When a female approaches, they get disturbed, and since they have x-ray vision, they can get aroused and frustrated!

Unlike in Jehangir's time, these days, there are plenty of men inside and outside the tomb who would gladly take your money!

Pen is mightier than the sword

The Mall Road of Lahore was built in the British times. The purpose was to connect the old cantonment in Anarkali area with the new cantonment in Mian Mir area. The 5-mile-long road was lined with trees providing shade from the scorching sun and became popular as *Thandi Sarak* (The cool street) among the locals. In those days when Lahore was compared to Paris, it was a favourite place for the beautiful and fashionable elite of the city to stroll in the evening, and this also made it cool in the modern use of this term.

Many important government and cultural buildings were and are along this thoroughfare, which unfortunately is now jam-packed with cars and no longer fit for a pleasure stroll. Although statues of humans are frowned upon among the Muslims, along the Mall, no less than 5 statues were built during the British days. These were:

1. Queen Victoria at Charing Cross. She was the longest-running British monarch till Queen Elizabeth and the first monarch of India.

2. John Lawrence in front of the High Court. Lawrence, as the administrator of Lahore after it was annexed by the

British, played a major role in the development of the city. Later, he also served as the Governor-General of India.

3. Lala Lajpat Rai near *Zumzma Gun*. A prominent anti-colonial politician known as the 2nd lion of Punjab (Ranjit Singh being the first). It was the death of Rai due to injuries sustained in a police baton charge during a peaceful protest in Lahore that incited Bhaghat Singh and his associates to plan the killing of the police officer responsible for ordering the action.

4. Ganga Ram near the Lahore Museum. A prominent engineer, architect, and philanthropist who built many of the buildings along the Mall as well as Model Town (and thus the new Lahore).

5. Alfred Woolner outside Punjab University. Unlike other high achievers, just a Sanskrit scholar.

Yet out of the above, only one statue survives to this day. The statue of the Queen has been removed to the basement of Lahore Museum, Lawrence's has been relocated to Ireland, and Ganga Ram and Lajput Rai's statues were destroyed by mobs during the partition riots. Only the statue of the scholar remains intact! Perhaps because the public at large does not know who he was and has no reason to dislike him.

I wonder if the realization that he was a scholar of the language of Hindus can prompt demands of it be removed as well or maybe one day a Wahabi/Takfiri terrorist may decide to blow it away , but at the moment, it has by outlasting monarchs, governors, politicians, and mega-rich builders proved that people of knowledge leave longer-lasting imprints than people of power and/or wealth.

In her book "Fallen Idols: Twelve Statues That Made History," the historian Alex Tunzelmann narrates the stories of 12 statues of historical figures that were destroyed or damaged during the George Floyd protests of 2020. However, I am sure just like the statue of Woolner was spared, the statues of scholars would have survived these riots as well.

Woolner, who graduated from Trinity College, Oxford, came to Lahore in 1903 aged 25, and joined the Punjab University as its registrar. In 1928, he became the Vice-Chancellor of the University, a post he held till his death in 1936. His widow Mary died in 1944 and as per her will, their entire estate was bequeathed to Punjab University. Woolner rests in the *Gora Qabristan* in Lahore.

He who has not seen Wazir Khan Mosque has not seen Lahore

Easily the most beautiful mosque in Lahore which has been described as a beauty spot (mole) on the face of the city. After entering the city through Delhi gate, the mosque can be reached by going straight through the narrow and busy Kashmiri Bazar. Here, there is a prominent spice market and the aroma of spices will entertain your senses.

The mosque is a Mughal building but was not built by a Mughal king. This credit goes to a man called Sheikh Ilm-ud-Din Ansari who was originally a Hakim (physician) from Chiniot.

The legend says that he came into the limelight when Queen Noor Jehan, the beloved of Emperor Jehangir, developed an abscess or something on the sole of her foot. This was painful to walk on, but she was so embarrassed that she wanted a physician to treat it without looking at it or touching it! Also, treatment failure was to be punished by death, so no one dared but Hakim Ansari did.

He first filled a hole in the floor with wet mud and asked the queen to step through it. After that, by studying the footprint, he was able to localize the lump and diagnose what it was. He then placed a tiny sharp blade or something at the spot where the lump was, and the queen was asked to walk over it and then walk briskly for a few minutes. The abscess was thus punctured, providing the queen instant relief from pain, and as she walked around, all the puss etc. got squeezed out. She was so pleased that Hakim Sahib became a millionaire.

He also became a close friend and physician of Prince Khurram, who became the emperor Shah Jehan. When Shah Jehan's favourite wife Mumtaz Mahal died in Burhanpur, Hakim Ansari was entrusted with taking her body for burial in Agra 1000 kilometres away. Eventually, Hakim Ansari became the governor of Lahore and was known as Wazir Khan. He used his own money to build the mosque named after him, and it took 7 years for it to be completed, under his personal supervision (1634 to 1641)

The striking feature of the Mosque is the use of glazed mosaic tiles and frescoes both outside and inside. This is a common feature of Mosques and tombs in Iran and Central Asia but quite rarely seen in the subcontinent. In fact, it is only in Punjab and Sind that buildings have this ornamentation, and curiously although these were built in Mughal times, they were not built by the monarch himself but by princes and nobles of his court. Some architects call this Lahore-specific architecture in the Indian Subcontinent, and nowhere in this region can one find a better example than Wazir Khan Mosque.

The art on the walls is considered so important that John Lockwood Kipling, who was the first director of Mayo College of Art (now called National College of Art), made all his students spend time studying it. According to him, this is one of the few examples of real Fresco art (Buono Fresco) in the world. Known as Kashi Kari, this is an elaborate process of preparing very thin tiles. It involves first preparing a paste by mixing sand, lime, and powdered glass with rice water (Khamir). These are cut to size and dried. After that, a liquid mix of lime and lead or powdered glass and lead called *astar* is spread over this. Finally, pounded glass is mixed with extract of certain plants to prepare what is named *kanch* and spread over. The tile is then baked till the glass fuses and then attached to the plastered wall.

No wonder the Mosque catches the imagination of writers who have based their stories in Lahore, the most well-known of them being John Kipling's famous son, Rudyard Kipling. It was while he was living in Lahore that Kipling published his first collection of short stories, and the very first story, "The Gate of a Hundred Sorrows," describes the location of an opium den within 100 yards of Wazir Khan Mosque. In another of his stories titled "City of Dreadful Night," he describes people sleeping like dead (probably intoxicated) in the square in front of the Mosque, and one had to walk with care so as not to step on them. The story ends with the narrator, no doubt Kipling himself as he was known to wander the narrow streets of Lahore during the summer nights, taking refuge from the heat in a minaret of the Mosque till the call for the morning prayer is delivered.

Years later at the age of 42, Kipling became the first English language writer and, at that time, the youngest recipient of a Noble prize for literature.

Kipling's writings no doubt inspired the great Argentinian Spanish writer Jorge Borges who was blind and for sure never visited Lahore. Despite this, his short story "Blue Tiger," written in 1977, starts and ends in Lahore. Based in 1904, the central character is a Scotsman who has moved to Lahore and works as a professor at the Punjab University (Borges wrote University of Lahore but we can forgive him for that). The story is about mysterious self-multiplying blue stones that bring the narrator to the brink of insanity and ends at the Wazir Khan Mosque as he writes, "Inside the mosque, it occurred to me that God and Allah are two names for a single, Inconceivable Being, and I prayed aloud that I be freed from my burden." His prayers are answered as a blind beggar takes the stones from him and tells him that one who does not give all gives nothing.

Borges did not base this scene in the Wazir Khan Mosque at random, he knew the benefits Sufi mystics ascribed to insanity, allowing them to unburden themselves from the demands of the physical world and devote totally to God. And most certainly he chose Lahore knowing the city's association with Sufi mystics who preached a religion of universal tolerance and love.

No wonder within Wazir Khan Mosque are the graves of not one but two Sufi Mystics.

There is a famous saying, 'He who has not seen Lahore is not born' and I would add, 'He who has not seen Wazir Khan Mosque has not seen Lahore.'

Sir Ganga Ram

I have previously mentioned the 5 statues that were situated in Lahore. Three of these were of English people, those who had colonized India, and two belonged to native Indians: these were Lala Lajpat Rai and Sir Ganga Ram. Besides the fact that both of them were Indians, Hindus, and Punjabis, they shared a strong bond with the city of Lahore although neither was born in Lahore. However, apart from these common traits, in a way, they were poles apart from each other. Lajpat Rai was an ardent activist in the Indian freedom movement, which demanded an end to the British Raj, while Ganga Ram can be best described as a loyal servant of the Raj. Yet there is no other person who has done more for Lahore in recent history than Ganga Ram. Here let me briefly run through how the tide of fortune affected Lahore over the years.

Although it was briefly the capital of the Ghaznavid Empire, Lahore was no more than a dilapidated provincial city before Akbar moved the capital of the Mughal Empire to Lahore in 1584. I am sure besides other reasons the move must have been influenced by the tradition of religious tolerance prevalent in Lahore, which would have suited

Akbar's idea of a pluralistic religion. Akbar's successors Jehangir and Shah Jehan stalled this process, but Lahore achieved the pinnacle of its glory during this time. Shah Jehan shifted the capital back to Delhi, which was a setback for Lahore, but his favourite son Dara Shikoh became the governor of Lahore and kept the city thriving. Dara was also a Sufi-mystic and wrote books that showed the similarity between Islam and Vedic religions if practiced with guides like Mian Mir.

It is possible that if in the subsequent power struggle, Dara had won, he would have shifted the capital back to Lahore and pursued the development of a pluralistic religion. Alas, it was the puritanical Aurangzeb who won and killed Dara. He then built the monstrous Badshahi Mosque as a symbol of his authority, but for many years no one prayed there as the people of Lahore boycotted something built over the dead body of their beloved prince. Lahore went into decline after that, and although it became the capital of Ranjit Singh's empire in the 19th century, its fortunes did not change that much as Ranjit Singh promoted Amritsar over Lahore. No major architectural projects were executed during his time except the Hazori Bagh in the Fort and a few havelis of court officials and princes. Many of the Mughal era buildings suffered as marble and wood were removed to build Sikh religious buildings in Amritsar.

The British annexed Lahore in 1849. The first census in Punjab under the British showed its population to be less than that of Amritsar. The British decided to create a new Lahore as a symbol of the British-Indian empire, and here we come to the brilliant Ganga Ram who was the executive engineer of Lahore for 12 years and built most of the buildings on the Mall Road, Lahore's Champs Elysees, as well as the new residential area Model Town outside the walled city. In this, he received significant assistance from the architect Bhai Ram Singh who had studied at the Mayo School of Arts (Now National College of Arts) under John Kipling. Today when we think of Lahore, it is the part outside the walled city that comes to mind, and in fact, all this is new Lahore built to a major degree by Sir Ganga Ram who can be considered the father of modern Lahore.

Curiously, even those who lament British Colonialism and what it did to India, are full of praise for Sir Ganga Ram and what he did for Lahore. Please note that this is in no way a slight on Sir Ganga Ram who financed many of the philanthropy projects out of his pocket, but the fact remains that without the knowledge and skills he acquired in Bradford and without the support of the British, he would not have been able to give so much to Lahore that he did as an engineer employed by the Raj.

Sir Ganga Ram also reminds us of the paradoxical relationship between Lahore and the non-Muslim inhabitants of this city. In 1947, the city was ethnically cleansed of all Hindus and Sikhs; however, what people of these religions had built in Lahore stayed, like Sir Ganga Ram Hospital, which is one of the main teaching hospitals of Lahore. This is illustrated in the story by Sadat Hasan Manto where a man attacking the statue of Sir Ganga Ram gets injured and goes to Sir Ganga Ram for treatment!

The riddle of Malik Ayaz

Tucked away on a busy road in Rang Mahal (Palace of Colour), Lahore, is the tomb of Malik Ayaz. When I visited it, the flower seller outside described it as the grave of the first Muslim governor of Punjab. Lahore first came under the rule of a Muslim king in 1021 when Mahmood of Ghazni captured it after a prolonged siege. The relationship between Mahmood and Ayaz is well known and made popular by Iqbal's famous verse, *"Aik he saf mein kharay ho gaye Mahmood o Ayaz"* intending to highlight the absence of class/cast divisions in Islamic society where a slave and his master can pray side by side.

Ayaz is believed to be a Georgian slave who became the favorite of Mahmood. It is narrated by various sources, including the recent book by Talbot and Kamran on Lahore, that Ayaz was the first governor of Lahore appointed by Mahmood before he returned to Ghazni and he stayed in Lahore till his death in 1041, building the walled city and the fort.

While the above is widely accepted, it is challenged with sound argument by Majid Sheikh Sahib, who tells us that historians of that time like Gardezi mention Ayaz as

Mahmood's "Lakhtay," which is a polite word for the rude "londa (boy partner)". So why should the Sultan return to Ghazni leaving his favourite lakhtay in Lahore, he asks. It is also known that Ayaz was present in Ghazni when Mahmood died in 1030 and bathed his body to prepare it for burial.

Furthermore, Majid Sheikh names a succession of governors appointed by Mahmood to administer Lahore, including Abdullah Qiratigin, Abul Fath of Damghan, Abul Farj of Kirman, and Aryaruq in the years following 1021. There is no mention of Ayaz in Lahore during this time. It is only many years after the death of Mahmood in 1037 that Ayaz, now elevated to a Malik, arrives in Lahore as advisor to the appointed governor Majdud, son of the then Sultan Masud. And indeed, he did stay there till 1041 when he died mysteriously.

As the wall around Lahore was built around the same time, Malik Ayaz can be credited with that, but it looks like he was not the first Muslim governor of Punjab. In fact, he was never a governor and only an advisor, though with Majdud being very young, Ayaz is thought to have been running the show.

The Gun

Depending on from which side you are coming, you will find this gun at the start or the end of Lahore's famous Mall Road. One of its names is Bhangian de Tope (cannon of Bhangies). Bhangi was one of the Hindu jati of untouchables who were only allowed one profession, to clean latrines. After the British came, most of them converted to Christianity, but most kept the same profession. Some people think the gun got this name because of the large population of Christians, aka Bhangis, in this area. The actual reason for the name is a bit different.

The gun was made in 1757 in Lahore by an officer of Afghan king Ahmed Shah Durrani (Abdali). The Afghans had captured Lahore only recently, and the citizens were asked to surrender their kitchen utensils to extract the brass and copper required for the construction of the gun.

Actually, two guns were made of the same size, both almost 14.5 feet long with a bore of 9.5 inches, making them the biggest guns in India, perhaps the world, at that time. Not much is known about the other gun, but this one was named Zamzama by Durrani, meaning Thunder.

In 1761, Durrani used both guns in the third battle of

Panipat, which dealt a decisive blow to Maratha power in north India. Ironically, the kitchen utensils confiscated from many Hindu households were used in the construction of the guns used to defeat the biggest Hindu military empire of that time.

While returning to Kabul after the battle, the victorious Afghan army was faced with the problem of arranging transport for the 22,000 Maratha women and children they had enslaved, and so this gun was left at Lahore. The other gun was with the army and was lost while crossing the Chenab river. Before the Afghans could transport Zamzama, a Sikh Chieftain Harri Singh attacked Lahore and captured the gun. Harri Singh was the head of a Sikh state which was called Bhangi Misl, centered around Amritsar. How it got this name is not clear, but it is said it was because of the addiction of its founder to Bhang, an intoxicating form of hashish quite popular among mystics and sadhus.

Hari Singh renamed the gun as Bhangianwali Tope. Over the next 40 years, the gun changed hands several times before it was captured by Ranjit Singh in 1802, who used it in five battles, in the last it got badly damaged and was retired. After moving around a few times, it found its final resting place in front of the Lahore Museum in 1870.

Nowadays, it is most widely known as Kim's Gun, yet this has never been an official name for it!

When Rudyard Kipling published his novel Kim in 1900-01, the gun gained widespread literary fame as the novel starts with the passage, "He sat in defiance of municipal orders, astride the gun Zam-Zammeh, on her old platform, opposite the old Ajaibgher, the Wonder House, as the natives called the Lahore Museum. Who holds Zam-Zammah, that 'fire-breathing dragon', hold the Punjab, for the great green-bronze piece is always first of the conqueror's loot."

The novel's hero, a thirteen-year-old orphan named Kim, thus gave the gun its unofficial name.

Amrita and Sahir: A love story from Lahore

Amrita Pritam is one of the most acclaimed female Punjabi poets of all time, loved and admired on both sides of the border. Amrita, who was born in Gujranwala and spent her youth in Lahore, was not just a talented poet but also a strikingly beautiful woman, about whom the film writer C.L. Kavish wrote, "Amrita Pritam was a chiselled piece of marble. If a sculptor's eyes had fallen on her, he would have carved a statue out of her that would have been worshipped as Radha in temples today."

Praised all over the subcontinent, the winner of many prestigious awards, Amrita had no shortage of money and spent the last 40 or so years of her life with a man who worshipped the very ground she walked on. It can be said that she achieved all that is possible in life, but she did not get what she most desired. Amrita did not get Sahir Ludhianvi, with whom she was totally, madly, and desperately in love. Amrita and Sahir's love story is one of the strangest and tragically beautiful tales of our times. Curiously, we know almost nothing about this love from Sahir's side; all we know is from what Amrita has written in her poems, stories, and memories.

Amrita first met Sahir in 1940 when she was 21 and already married, and he was 19. The venue was a place appropriately named Preet Nagar (The Land of Love) midway between Lahore and Ludhiana, where a mushaira (poetry recitation) was being held, and Sahir, who had recently created a name with his poem Taj Mahal, was one of the poets. For Amrita, it was preet (love) at first sight. "I do not know whether it was the magic of his words or his silent gaze, but I was captivated by him," she recalled later.

It does not seem that young Sahir took much notice of her at that time. The function ended after midnight, and the plan was for the participants to walk to another village called Lopki the next morning to catch a bus for Lahore. Due to rain, the conditions were slippery, and everyone had to walk slowly and cautiously. Amrita thought this was destiny working for her as she walked some distance behind Sahir and kept watching him and his shadow. Later on, she wrote, "At that time, I didn't know I would spend so many scorching years of my life walking in his shadow or that at times I would get tired and seek solace in my own words.These words were from those poems which I had written in Sahir's love, but I never revealed the inspiration behind them publicly."

As time passed, they met in other literary gatherings and became friendly with each other, but Sahir was still blind to the love Amrita was growing in her heart. Also, there was the question of distance, for Sahir was studying in Ludhiana and Amrita, since her marriage, was living in Lahore around 35 miles away.

Then in 1943, fate intervened. Sahir was forced to leave Government College Ludhiana, and he moved to Lahore. This was the time when love between Sahir and Amrita blossomed in the vibrant, multicultural, multi-ethnic Lahore of pre-partition days. Amrita, whose husband Preetam Singh had a large shop in Anarkali bazar, lived in a house on Dhani Ram Road. If we follow this road east, it curves south in front of King Edward Medical College to become Ewing Road, which goes past *Neela Gombad* (Blue Dome) fountain to join Mall Road, the Champs-Élysées of Lahore in those days.

Is it possible that the two lovebirds would take a tonga to the Mall and stroll hand in hand, or go to nearby Anarkali for the famous chat? Unlikely, for I doubt times were so liberal at that time, and after all, Amrita was a married woman. However, there is no doubt that the two did meet in private regularly, and the venue was Amrita's house.

Sahir once again is silent on these events, but Amrita later wrote, 'Sahir also told me, much later in life, "When both of us were in Lahore, I would often come close to your house and stand at the corner where I would sometimes buy a paan, or light a cigarette, or hold a glass of soda in my hand. I would stand there for hours together watching that window of your house which opened towards the street."'

I wonder what Preetam Singh was doing at this time. Is it possible that Sahir was watching the house, waiting for the hubby to leave? We will never know.

In her autobiography *Rasidi Ticket* (Revenue Stamp), which was published when Amrita was in her 50s, she frequently mentions her obsession for Sahir. About these meetings, she writes, 'When Sahir used to come to meet me in Lahore, it was as if an extension of my silence had occupied the adjacent chair and then gone away. He would quietly smoke his cigarettes, putting out each after having finished only half of it and lighting a new one. I wanted to feel the touch of his hand, but in front of me were the restrictions of my marriage which I could not ignore. After he would leave, the ashtray would be full of his unfinished cigarettes... I would keep these remaining cigarettes carefully in the cupboard after he left. I would only light them while sitting alone by myself. When I would hold one of these cigarettes between my fingers, I would feel as if I was touching his hands... That is how I became a smoker, but I never told Sahir about this.'

So apparently, it was a chaste and platonic relationship. Still, early in 1945, Amrita, who had been married for eight years, became pregnant for the first time. She imagined the child, a son, growing inside her who looked like Sahir (or so she wished), and when her son Navraj was born, he did resemble Sahir! So much so that according to Amrita, when he was 13, Navraj asked her, *"Mama, such batain, kya mein Sahir uncle ka baita hoon?* (Mama, please tell the truth, am I Sahir Uncle's son)?" Amrita said no and was able to convince him. She always maintained that the resemblance was not genetic but due to her imagination which had shaped the child's features when he was in her womb! Can this be possible? Well, your guess is as good as mine.

1945 was also the year when 'Talkhian' the first poetry collection by Sahir was published. This brought him fame and recognition. Sahir, whose father was a serial polygamist and is said to have married 14 women, had treated his mother (wife no 4) badly and so she had left him when Sahir was 13. The father tried to get custody of the boy but failed and threatened to kill him. Due to this, Sahir had spent a deprived life and now as he was made the editor of two magazines he was able to earn some money.

Amrita and Sahir's tranquil world changed in 1947 when vicious riots erupted in Lahore, as Amrita wrote later,

'In 1947 Lahore was turned into a graveyard. It was the politics of hate that swept Lahore in flames; at night one would see houses in flames, hear cries of desperation, and witness long hours of curfew during the day. Expecting my second child, I often went for a walk on the Mall road, there one day I saw a Sikh running around, with a knife pierced into his stomach. I rushed back and never stepped out of my house again. At night I would watch Lahore burning from my rooftop and think, 'does this land not belong to those who were born here? For whom are those spears flashing in their hands?'

Amrita and her family moved to India. According to Amrita, there was no intention to migrate, and the move was purely due to the fact that she needed medical attention, and no doctors or midwives were available in the riot-torn city. In her mind, Amrita was sure that this insanity would soon pass, and she would be able to return.

Alas, this was not so. By winter, it was clear to her that there would be no going back to her beloved Lahore.

Sahir, who had gone to Bombay early in 1947, returned to Lahore probably around the time that Amrita was leaving. He stayed in Lahore till 1949, but then when a case was registered against him for his left-wing ideas after he published a poem called *Awaz a Adam*, he left for India, moving for a short while to Delhi and then settling in Bombay to become the most sought-after songwriter of Indian movies, the Javed Akhtar of his days.

Although both Amrita and Sahir ended up becoming Indian citizens, it looks as if the loss of their connection with Lahore and the end of the multi-ethnic religiously diverse world of pre-partition India created a schism between them that could not be repaired. Both believed in a universal humanity as Sahir tells us in one of his songs:

Malik nain her insan ko insan banya
Ham nein usay Hindu ya Musalman banaya
Qudrat neing tu bakhshi thi humanin eik he dharti
Ham nein kahin Bharat kahin Iran banaya
Creator made every human just a human
We made some Hindu and some Muslim
God gave us just one earth
We made somewhere India and somewhere Iran

Sentiments, Amrita voices when she tells us about her childhood rebellion against the segregation of drinking glasses into Muslim and Hindu at her home.

Once religious dogmatism eliminated the grey area of mutual acceptance, they had nowhere to go. That is why, despite meeting on and off during the remaining years of Sahir's life, Amrita moved on to Imroz while Sahir never married or had a partner.

Amrita made Sahir the focus of many of her poems and stories and openly acknowledged this. She writes when she got a national award in 1956 that she did not feel much joy as the person for whom she had written the poem that won the award was indifferent to it. In one of her poems, she describes such later meetings with Sahir:

After many years, a sudden meeting
Both of us experienced a kind of nervousness
A whole night stretched ahead of us
But one half of the poem remained confined in one corner
The other half, in another
Then, the next morning
We met like torn pieces of paper
I took his hand in my hand
And he put his arm through mine
And we both laughed liked censors

And then putting the piece of paper on a cold table
We scratched out the entire poem written on it

In her book Rasidi Ticket, Amrita describes an occasion when she says she felt like a pure woman with nothing of a writer inside her. She writes, "Once when Sahir came to visit me, he had a sore throat and tightness in his chest... That day I massaged a cooling balm on his throat and chest... I kept doing this for a long time... And I felt that like this, standing on my feet and rubbing his chest gently with my pores, my fingers, and my palms, I can spend my entire life. I don't need any pen or paper."

Shortly before her death and not in good health, she wrote a poem called Mein teenu phair milan gi (I will meet you again) dedicated to her much younger partner the painter Imroze. I think at least some of the lines are for Sahir:

'Or maybe I will come back as a spring
And from the life currents of this spring
I will take drops of water
and rub them on your chest
and like a balm of coolness
I will sooth your burning chest
I do not know anything else
but I do know this much
that whatever time will do
In this life you will walk with me'

It is possible Amrita was the inspiration for many of Sahir's poems and songs; however, he never acknowledged this publicly.

Progressive Writers Association

بیتیں گے کبھی تو دن آخر یہ بھوک کے اور بیکاری
ٹوٹیں گے کبھی تو بت آخر دولت کی اجارہ داری کے
جب ایک انوکھی دنیا کی بنیاد اٹھائی جائے گی
وہ صبح کبھی تو آئے گی

The days of hunger and unemployment will end one day
The control of wealth by the selected few will end one day
When the foundation of an amazing new world will be laid
That dawn will surely come one day

(Sahir Ludihanvi)

The dream and hope of a more egalitarian and fairer world gained traction in the aftermath of the French Revolution and gave birth to the Socialist movements in Europe. Besides other things, the colonialists brought these socialist ideas to the Indian subcontinent, which since antiquity has had mega-scale inequalities based on birth and wealth among its large population.

In 1932, a group of Indian writers published a collection of short stories titled *Angaray* (Burning Embers). The book was soon banned by the government after protests from the civil and religious authorities. The stories attacked the hypocrisy of a society that kept a taboo on mentioning certain social evils that the so-called decent people felt should be kept hidden under the carpet. Following this, these writers thought of starting a league of like-minded progressive writers. However, Sajad Zaheer, who was one of this group, was sent by his family to go to London to study law while things cooled down in India. There he came in contact with several like-minded Indian writers of the diaspora who first met in the backroom of a Chinese restaurant in Denmark Street and launched the Indian Progressive Writers Association in London. In 1935, Sajad Zaheer returned to India and started work on setting up the association in India by traveling to various Indian cities to meet the local writers and get their support. In this way, the branches of the association were set up in various Indian cities, including Lahore. Many prominent poets and writers of that day like Faiz Ahmed Faiz, Krishan Chandar, Sibt Hassan, Ali Sardar Jafery, Sahir Ludhianvi, Sadat Hasan Manto, etc., were active members.

The basic principle of the movement was that art should never be for art's sake and must play an active role in bringing about social change for the better. The movement was anti-colonial, anti-feudal, anti-capitalist, and anti-religious; in other words, it was against all systems used to oppress humans, and its members exposed and attacked the exploitation of farmers, workers, women, etc., through their writings.

After partition, it split into PWA-Hindustan and PWA-

Pakistan as members moved in one direction or the other. In Pakistan, Lahore became the center of PWA, and the first All Pakistan PWA convention was held at Lawrence Gardens Lahore in November 1949. The movement had many enemies in Lahore, including the writer-journalist Shorish Kashmiri, who accused it of being anti-Pakistan, while a group of ulema declared it anti-Islam. Considering the writers of PWA to be a threat to the feudal lords, factory owners, and religious leaders who led the government of Pakistan, a campaign of intimidation, harassment, and occasional physical violence was started against its members.

Some of the writers were unable to survive in this atmosphere. The leading progressive poet Sahir Ludhianvi published a poem "Awaz-e-Adam" (Voice of Adam):

> *dabegī kab talak āvāz-e-ādam ham bhī dekheñge*
> *rukeñge kab talak jazbāt-e-barham ham bhī dekheñge*
> *chalo yūñhī sahī ye jaur-e-paiham ham bhī dekheñge*
> *dar-e-zindāñ se dekheñ yā urūj-e-dār se dekheñ*
> *tumheñ rusvā sar-e-bāzār-e-ālam ham bhī dekheñge*
> *zarā dam lo ma.āl-e-shaukat-e-jam ham bhī dekheñge*
> *ye zo.am-e-quvvat-e-faulād-o-āhan dekh lo tum bhī*
> *ba-faiz-e-jazba-e-īmān-e-mohkam ham bhī dekheñge*
> *jabīn-e-kaj-kulāhī khaak par kham ham bhī dekheñge*
> *mukāfāt-e-amal tārīkh-e-insāñ kī rivāyat hai*
> *karoge kab talak nāvak farāham ham bhī dekheñge*
> *kahāñ tak hai tumhāre zulm meñ dam ham bhī dekheñge*
> *ye hañgām-e-vidā-e-shab hai ai zulmat ke farzando*
> *sahar ke dosh par gulnār parcham ham bhī dekheñge*

tumheñ bhī dekhnā hogā ye aalam ham bhī dekheñge

How long will you suppress the voice of man we will see as well,
How long will the angry people control their emotions we will see as well,
If it is going to be this way then this period of time we will see as well,
Weather we see from the jail or from where we are hanged,
Your humiliation in the whole world we will see as well,
Just wait the pride of kings rubbed in dirt we will see as well,
Look at these strong arms of steel and iron,
The power of complete faith we will see as well,
The proud heads bowed in the dust we will see as well,
To answer for your actions is a tradition of human history,
How long will you make excuses to escape justice we will see as well,
How much power is in your oppression we will see as well,
These uproars celebrate passing of the night o children of darkness,
In the morning breeze the red flag we will see as well,
You will have to see as well and this time we will see as well.

Following this, arrest warrants were issued against him, and he quit Pakistan for good, moving to India. Other writers like Faiz Ahmed Faiz and Sajad Zaheer, who did not listen to the threats, were implicated in the Rawalpindi Conspiracy case, and while Zaheer, like Sahir, escaped to

India, Faiz spent many years under trial and detention.

The PWA itself contributed to its decline by becoming totally devoted to the USSR in whom they saw nothing wrong, realists like Manto did not toe this line and were attacked by PWA.

In 1954, PWA was banned and went underground. It was revived under the socialist government of ZA Bhutto in 1971.

In Lahore, a cafe on Mall Road, which was renamed from India Tea House to Pak Tea House, has been the watering hole for Lahori intellectuals belonging to PWA. As progressive writing and thinking in specific, and intellectual activities in general, are discouraged by the Pakistani establishment, the PWA and Pak Tea House have become just a shell of their past glory. Still, PWA is alive and holds its meetings regularly at Pak Tea House, and some I have attended during my various trips to Lahore. Unfortunately, PWA Lahore has been split into two rival groups who hold their meetings on different days.

Lahore Fort

Within Lahore Fort, among other things, we have the sleeping chambers of the emperors Jehangir and Shah Jahan. Jehangir's (now a museum) is much larger, perhaps because Lahore was one of his capitals or to accommodate his well-known fondness for women. In front of the chamber, which Jehangir would have emerged from after an opium-assisted sleep, is a large garden with fountains that would be running in those days, with peacocks roaming about. A bit further down is Shah Jahan's bedroom. He was born in Lahore but moved the capital to Delhi. His bedchamber is much smaller, after all, it was only him and Mumtaz Mahal. Coming out of his chamber in the morning, what he would have seen is a decent-sized swimming pool which formed part of a garden where only women were allowed. So while the emperor was faithful to Mumtaz, the love of his life, he could at least feast his eyes on nubile young slave girls splashing around in the pool. As they say, "It is good to be the king."

The Lahore Fort is an imposing structure. No one really knows how old this fort is. It is thought to pre-date the Delhi Sultanate; however, the first king to initiate a major construction project in the fort was Akbar, who lived here, on and off, for 12 years. The popular love story of Anarkali and Prince Salim took place within the walls of this fort. Even if the story was true (which it almost certainly is not), still the fabulous scene from Mughal-e-Azam where Anarkali dances in the Shish Mahal (The Mirror Palace) could not have taken place, for the Shish Mahal in Lahore Fort was built by Emperor Shah Jahan much later when Salim (Emperor Jehangir) was long dead.

Hardly any of the Akbar era construction in the Fort has survived, perhaps due to a fire which destroyed a lot of structures in 1597, and so most of Mughal architecture in the fort is from the time of Jehangir and Shah Jahan. Within the premises of the fort is the Samadhi of Maharaja Ranjeet Singh, whom the secular-minded Punjabis consider the first Punjabi ruler of Punjab, as well as of the fifth Sikh Guru Arjan, who compiled Guru Granth Sahib, the sacred book of Sikhs. According to legend, Guru Arjan was a close personal friend of Mian Mir, the patron saint of Lahore. It was at this fort that Guru Arjan was imprisoned by Emperor Jehangir, allegedly tortured, and then killed, although some claim that he disappeared (or drowned) in the river.

The persecution of Guru Arjan led to his son, the sixth Guru Har Gobind, changing Sikhism from a completely pacifist religious order to a martial culture, something that proved disastrous for the Mughals in particular and Muslims in general.

Although many of the Mughal-era buildings remain structurally intact, their interiors are not from the Mughal times. For example, the interior of Jehangir's bed-chamber is from the Sikh era, and so are the walls of the Shish Mahal, while the ceiling is Mughal. The only structure Aurangzeb, the last of the so-called Great Mughals, added to the fort is the Alamgiri gate, most likely as it provided the quickest way to get to the monstrosity called Badshahi Mosque he built as well.

The gate leads to a *Bradarri* and garden called *Hazoori Bagh*, built by Maharaja Ranjit Singh, which lies between Badshahi Mosque and Alamgiri Gate. In front of the Mosque is Iqbal's mausoleum. Once when I visited with my mother, uncle, and aunt, policemen stationed there told us not to go towards the mausoleum due to security concerns. They suggested we offer prayers for Iqbal from a distance but allowed us to walk around in the garden. My uncle could not walk anymore, so the police produced a chair for him to sit, and we strolled around. When we returned, a policeman came to us and said, "Come, I will take you to the mausoleum." As we walked towards it, he said to my mother, "I am sorry, we did not know you are Iqbal's relatives." I asked him how he knew that, and he said your uncle told us! He then said, "As you are his relatives, it is your right to visit his grave." At this, my mother remarked, "No, we don't have any special rights, and everyone has a right to visit it."

I asked him who he thinks wants to attack the mausoleum, expecting him to say RAW, but he said he does not know for sure but thinks it is the Taliban! The Mausoleum has verses in Persian on the ceiling. My mother translated one which read, "I had lighted my lamp from the fire on Mount Sinai, but they have hidden it in their pockets."

The British also used parts of the fort, the underground areas, as torture cum interrogation cells for those they did not like, for example, the freedom fighters. After the British departed, their colonialism stayed under the home-grown sahibs of Pakistan, and so did the use of torture cells. Many unfortunate political detainees were kept here in atrocious conditions and sometimes even murdered here, for example, Hasan Nasir. I am told this practice is still prevalent.

MAHARAJA RANJIT SINGH

During one of my visits to Lahore, I wanted to visit the samadhi (tomb) of Ranjit Singh, which is just a few yards from the main entrance of Lahore Fort. This is located inside a gurdwara, and a couple of plainclothes policemen were stationed at the gate. They asked me if I was Muslim, and when I said yes, they said, "Sorry, Muslims are not allowed to go in!" They would not tell me why. When I pleaded, I had come from England, they asked if I had my British passport on me, which of course I had left at home. They said, "Well, maybe if you had it with you, we could have let you in." I almost asked if they were afraid that Muslims will go in and convert, but more likely it is due to the possibility of a fanatic doing some violence inside. Either way, it is a sad situation.

It is a pity that the history books in Pakistan do not even mention Ranjit Singh, despite him being one of the few genuinely indigenous monarchs produced by the area that now comprises Pakistan. Ranjit Singh was born on 13 November 1780 in Gujranwala, Punjab! Those were turbulent times for Punjab, for in the last 50 years before that, the Mughal power had declined, and further to the east, the Afghan-Persian empire had revived. In 1739, Nadir Shah sacked Delhi, carrying away, besides thousands of women and children slaves, the peacock throne and Koh-a-Noor diamond. Not satisfied with this, the Afghan warlord Ahmad Shah Abdali raided Northern India multiple times through the 1750s and 60s. While Punjab was more of a thoroughfare for raiding Afghans, the fact that the Sikhs did not want Afghans, Mughals, or Persians to trample their land resulted in them being persecuted by all.

At the time of Ranjit's birth, Punjab was divided into multiple fiefdoms of various sizes ruled by Afghan and Sikh warlords. The Sikhs were divided into 12 *misls* (confederacies), all of which had feuds with each other. Ranjit's father was the leader of one of the smaller of these *misls, Sukerchakia*, based in Gujranwala. As he grew up, Ranjit was not a physically imposing presence. Short in stature and slightly built, he even suffered from the disability of having lost his right eye to smallpox! Still, what he lacked in physical strength, he made up for through his immense courage and intelligence.

Ranjit succeeded his father as the leader of the Sukechakia clan in 1792 at the tender age of just 12. He inherited the fortified city of Gujranwala, a militia of 5000 horsemen, and an alliance through marriage to Mehtab Kaur, daughter of the chief of Kanhayas misl. Without wasting any time, he went to work on consolidating and expanding his power. Lady luck also helped him while he established his kingdom as the rampant British were busy fighting the Central and Southern Indian powers like Marathas and Tipu Sultan. They did not come near Punjab until they annexed the areas around Delhi and Agra in 1803.

However, he had to deal with the other *misls*, the Marathas to the south, and the resurgent Afghan kingdom to the Northwest. His immediate rivals were the Bhangi clan who held Lahore and surrounded his territory on three sides. Over the next seven years, Ranjit fought a series of campaigns against Afghans and rival misls. In 1798, he took a second wife from another misl, and then in 1799, the same year as the British defeated Tipu Sultan, Ranjit announced himself to the wider world by capturing Lahore. The Bhangis then allied themselves with Pathan warlords of Kasur, and in 1801, after defeating them in the decisive battle of Bhasin, Ranjit proclaimed himself to be the Maharaja of Punjab with Lahore as his capital. Ranjit recruited able ministers to run his kingdom; he selected them on ability without concern for religion. His diwan (chief minister) was a Hindu, Ram Dhail; his commander-in-chief a Sikh, Fateh Singh, and foreign minister Azizuddin, a Muslim.

It was at this stage that the British noticed him. The Second Maratha War ended in 1804 and gave the East India Company control of the territory till the Sutlej River in the West, with Ranjit's kingdom beyond it. Over the previous five years of war, the British had established control over South, Central, and North India, with the Mughal king now just a puppet in their hands. However, the wars had created a mountain of debt, and the directors of the Company were not pleased at all and were demanding the resignation of the Governor-General Richard Wellesley. This situation was to Ranjit's advantage, as, at least for the time being, the British had no interest in further expansion Westwards. In 1804, Maratha Chieftain Jaswant Holkar appealed to Ranjit to join him against the British. Ranjit shrewdly declined, and in 1806, he signed a treaty with the British under which they agreed to keep out of Punjab as long as Ranjit did not enter into any alliance against them. Ranjit was now free to consolidate his power and expand it in Punjab. He gained control over Amritsar, Multan, and other smaller towns. Another treaty with the British in 1809 avoided a possible war and established that the Sutlej would be the boundary between them.

Ranjit was now free to concentrate on the Afghans who were always a threat. He reorganized his army on European lines and hired French and Italian generals. In 1813, Ranjit joined forces with an Afghan chieftain to march on Kashmir, where an ex-Afghan king, Shah Shujah, was being held prisoner. After Kashmir was captured, it was given to Afghan Barkzie brothers while Ranjit Singh got 9 lakh rupees and the Koh-i-Noor diamond, which was given to him by Shah Shujah's wife for freeing her husband. In 1818, he finally subdued Multan, which he had captured and lost several times. 1818-19 provided great opportunities due to disarray and civil war in Afghanistan. First, Ranjit captured Peshawar, though he gave it to an Afghan warlord in lieu of an annual payment, and then in July 1819, he annexed Kashmir, adding tax revenue of Rs 70 lakh per year to his treasury. His territories continued to expand; in 1823, the Afghans regrouped and attacked but were defeated in the battle of Tibbi Tehri near Naushera, in which Sikh fanatics, the Akalis, comprehensively outfought the Muslim fanatics, the Ghazis! In 1835, when one of his generals Zorawer Singh captured Ladakh, Ranjit's empire had reached its peak. By now, Ranjit's physical health was declining; he was increasingly using opium along with vast amounts of strong alcoholic spirits. In 1835, a British envoy Alexander Burns visited his darbar and was seated close to him; he commented that the Maharaja was 55 but looked 65. Although there were no new lands to conquer, Ranjit still had to deal with repeated rebellions, the most serious of which was the jihad by Sayyid Ahmed Barelvi from 1826-31.

Ranjit's last few years were spent shadow boxing with the British. His last masterful diplomatic coup was when, in 1839, the British decided to replace Dost Mohammad in Kabul with their pet Shah Shuja. They made a plan for this with Ranjit, and a Punjabi army was to do the job. But Ranjit maneuvered it in a way that, in the end, an all-British army was dispatched and did not enter his territory.

On June 27, 1839, Ranjit had a massive stroke and died while being attended by six European doctors. He was accompanied on his pyre by three of his Rajput wives and seven concubines. The ashes of all of them were, for some time, kept inside his samadhi, as well as the ashes of two pigeons who got caught up in the funeral pyre fire and were declared Sati!

A man with vision and farsightedness, Ranjit left a kingdom where everything seemed to be good. It had money, an annual income of 3 crore Rupees, a well-trained army, and a clearly defined line of succession for the next two generations. Yet, it disintegrated within 5 years of his death, once again proving the dictum that even the best-laid plans of mice and men often go completely wrong. The two main reasons for this were the low quality of his heirs, for one thing he could not do was to improve their abilities as rulers, and the second was the change in British policy who now wanted to expand

Westwards.

A lot can be written about Ranjit Singh as a ruler, and in many ways, he was the best despot one could ask for. Although his word was law, he rarely used his despotic powers and often acted after consulting with his ministers, whom he trusted to be able to run his kingdom. Though many Sikh writers are keen to point out the virtues of Sikh faith with Ranjit as an example, the fact is that though born a Sikh, Ranjit's personal conduct as a ruler was without any religious favouritism. He attended the religious festivals of all three major religions in his kingdom, gave charitable donations to Gurdwaras, Mosques, and Temples in equal proportions, and observed Moharrum, Dussehra, and Holi with the same devotion as Guru Nanak's birthday. In the same way, followers of all faiths were allowed to practice it without any hindrance in his kingdom.

Ranjit was an honest and shrewd monarch who, while not afraid to go to war, would rather avoid it by using diplomacy. He was free of most of the evils that absolute power brings; he did not have any rancour, paranoia, jealousy, and avarice. He remained humble throughout his life; he never wore any crown or regal ornamentations and insisted that everyone addresses him only as 'Singh Sahib'. One of the British officers who was his guest once and accidentally entered his bedchamber where he was resting has reported that it was a small room where the Maharaja was sleeping on an ordinary carpai!

Another remarkable quality he had was to forgive, even repeat offenders! Ranjit never ordered anyone to be killed as punishment. Rebellions were a common feature of those times, and Ranjit would deal with them with an iron hand, but only while the rebels were still fighting.

Once they were captured or surrendered, he would be magnanimous, invariably forgiving them and in most cases reinstating the rebel officer to his previous rank! Those who fought him bravely were treated with exceptional kindness and respect! An example is the Afghan warlord Muzaffar Khan who was holding Multan when Ranjit captured it in 1806. Ranjit made him his governor on payment of an annual tribute. Over the next 12 years, Muzaffar Khan raised the standard of rebellion at least 6 times, and each time he was defeated, forgiven, and reinstated. Finally, in 1818, during the last uprising, Muzaffar Khan and two of his sons were killed fighting bravely. Ranjit buried them with honor and wept with real tears.

The only two weaknesses he had were his fondness for alcohol and women. However, apparently, he always treated his women well. There are two misconceptions about Ranjit Singh. One is that he fought and resisted the British while in actual fact he avoided fighting them and was more of an ally to them. Some criticize him for not attacking the British; such criticism is unfair for Ranjit was never militarily strong enough to push the British out of India, and confronting them militarily would have been nothing but suicide. The other is the label of him being a Punjabi nationalist. Here the main problem is how to define Punjabi nationalism? As such, by far the single most important factor for this is Punjabi language, and Ranjit certainly did nothing to promote Punjabi in his kingdom. The language of his durbar and official business remained Persian! In the same way, the Sikh chieftains beyond Sutlej showed no desire to join his kingdom, preferring to become British subjects, once again showing that Punjabi nationalism did not find much of a champion in Ranjit Singh.

The war with the British that Ranjit had managed to avoid did not spare his final successor, youngest son Dalip Singh, who was just 6 at the time of the first Sikh war, 1845-46. The result was the loss of territory as well as the Koh-i-Noor, which had to be gifted to Queen Victoria, becoming part of the British crown jewels. Three years later, after the Second Sikh war, the British annexed his kingdom and deposed Dalip, who was banished from residing in Punjab. He was kept under house arrest at Fategarh where at age of 15 he converted to Christianity. The following year he was exiled to England where he is said to be treated with great affection by Queen Victoria. He in turn does not seem to be too fond of her for once after he was shown the Koh-i-Nur he examined it in complete silence and later in private called Victoria a common thief, no doubt he was referring to the theft of not just the diamond but his whole kingdom. Dalip eventually died in exile and none of his eight children had any offspring thus ending Ranjit's bloodline. It is rumoured that this infertility was due to chemicals given to them on orders of Victoria!

One legacy of Ranjit Singh's rule is the ongoing issue of Kashmir. As we know, Kashmir was part of his Kingdom. At the end of the First Sikh War, a large sum had been demanded by the British as indemnity for which there was no money in the treasury. At that time, Dogra Gulab Singh, who was the son of one of Ranjit's favorite servants, was in charge of Jammu and had quietly avoided being involved in the war while amassing a fortune. Here he came up with the idea that Maharaja Dalip, instead of money, gives Kashmir to the British, and he will then buy it from them. The deal was struck, and Kashmir became part of a new state of Jammu and Kashmir for a few lakh rupees. Had this not been the case and had Kashmir remained part of the Kingdom of Punjab, then three years later it would have been annexed by the British, becoming part of British India. Then, 100 years later, when India was partitioned, the fate of Kashmir would have been decided according to the partition plan, making it if not all, certainly Srinagar and the valley, automatically a part of Pakistan due to its overwhelming Muslim majority.

The Lion and the Peacock

At the time of his death at the age of 58, Ranjit Singh had 20 wives and 26 concubines in his harem, and while he was fond of all of them, it looks like the only woman he loved was the odd woman out! Moran (Female Peacock) was a *natch girl* (dancer/courtesan) from a village Makhanpura near Amritsar. Somehow, young Ranjit became her admirer. At that time, Ranjit had already married twice, but these were marriages of convenience for political reasons. His affair with Moran was due to real affection, as she was not from a noble Sikh or Rajput family and would not have brought Ranjit any political gain. Interestingly, this liaison was looked down upon by the families of both Ranjit and Moran. For Ranjit's clan, this was for obvious reasons; she was a dancing girl and a Muslim, and for Moran, her father did not want any serious relationship between her and a non-Muslim! So Ranjit built a *Bardari* midway between Lahore and Amritsar where he used to meet Moran. This place acquired the name of *Pull Kanjrian* (Bridge of courtesans), which Urdu/Hindi speakers will acknowledge as a derogatory term. It is now renamed as Pull Moran.

Soon after he was proclaimed the Maharajah of Punjab aged only 21, Ranjit married Moran! This was something that shocked everyone, for not only was he marrying a woman from a class considered only for fun and not marriage, but she was also a Muslim. As for Ranjit, this marriage was not just for love but also to elevate the status of dancing girls in society. The Sikh religious leaders did not accept this step by Ranjit, and he was ordered to present himself at Akal Takht in the Golden Temple. There he was told that he cannot be allowed to do what he has done and a punishment of 50 lashes was prescribed unless he repents and divorces Moran. Hearing this, Ranjit Singh took off his shirt and said, "Fine, I am ready for my punishment." Akali Phula Singh, the jathedar, could not bring himself to punish this courageous young man and changed the punishment to a fine.

Moran thus remained a favourite wife of Ranjit Singh. She lived in Lahore and patronized both mosques and temples. One such mosque was named Kanjri Masjid (now called Moran Masjid). However, she did not build a mosque or temple of any other religion as was the tradition among upper-class women. Instead, she built a school for girls so they could get education. Ranjit remained fond of her, which can be judged by the fact that while he never minted a coin in his name, he did one in the name of Moran Sarkar.

Rustam-a-Insanyat (Champion of Humanity)

Many years ago, an international tournament of *Desi Kushti* was held in Kohlapur district in India's Maharashtra state. Some wrestlers from Lahore were taking part, and a rumour spread that in one of the bouts, the great-grandson of *Gama Pehalvan* is taking part. Astonishingly, a crowd of 200,000 poor villagers stood in rain for 14 hours to catch a glimpse of this man only because of his heritage. The local newspaper declared, "The grandson of the God of Wrestling is coming." I am not sure if the grandson of the God did come, but it's unlikely that such an honour would have been reserved for even Sachin Tendulkar.

Ghulam Mohammed, known as Great Gama, was an incredible man and perhaps did have superhuman powers. Born in Amritsar to a Kashmiri family, he went on to win titles of Rustam-e-Hind (Champion of India) and Rustam-e-Zaman (Champion of the Universe). During a career of 50 years, he was never defeated, even though at 5 feet 7 inches, he was usually much shorter than his opponents.

His diet and exercise routine were legendary and included several gallons of milk, 3000 push-ups, and 5000 sit-ups every day! The famous martial arts star Bruce Lee acknowledged his respect for The Great Gama and claimed that he had adopted parts of his diet and exercise routine in his own training. Among his legendary accomplishments was when he challenged the top 12 wrestlers of Europe and America to a bout on the same day and one after the other defeated them all, none lasting more than a few minutes!

Early in 1947, with the fire of hate spreading through Punjab, Gama Sahib was living on Mohni Road in Lahore. He told the Hindus of his *Mohalla* that if they are attacked, he will defend them with his life, and when one day a mob approached the community, Gama Sahib stood in front of them with all of his group of wrestlers. As the leading hooligan came near, a slap from Gama Sahib sent him flying, and the rest ran away never to come again. A few days later, Gama Sahib escorted all the Hindus to the border where, with tears streaming from his eyes, he bade them goodbye, giving them one week's food from his own money.

Unfortunately, towards the end of his life, he struggled financially and is rather unknown among the present generation of Pakistani youth, despite the fact that he is the great-grandfather of Kalsoom Nawaz, the deceased wife of Nawaz Sharif.

Bradlaugh Hall

Bradlaugh Hall still stands as an imposing building, despite its neglected and dilapidated condition. It is under the administration of the Evacuees Property Board, which is supposed to look after it. However, besides slapping Quranic verses on its forehead after the creation of Pakistan to convert it into a Muslim building, it has been abandoned to rot, with all entrance points shuttered and locked. It seems like no one knows what to do with it, as despite its rich history, the building does not fit in with the official narrative of Lahore or Pakistan's history.

Charles Bradlaugh (1833-1891) was a British politician and activist, a secularist who advocated for trade unionism, universal suffrage, and republicanism. He is responsible for the change in British law whereby when taking an oath in parliament or a court of law, it is no longer required to swear on the Bible (or any other religious book). Charles Bradlaugh was a supporter of the Indian people's right to self-rule.

It was Bradlaugh's close friend and associate, Annie Besant, who started the Home Rule League in India, the first movement demanding self-rule by Indians.

When the Indian National Congress decided to hold its

1893 session in Lahore, it was decided to build a building for this purpose. On completion, it was named after Charles Bradlaugh, which was appropriate considering the secular and all-inclusive society Lahore had in those days.

It was also Bradlaugh Hall where the 1929 session of the Congress was held, at the end of which the long-running debate between Indian doves asking for autonomy within the Empire and hawks asking for full freedom was finally settled in favor of the latter. Following this, on December 31, 1929, at dawn, a flag of independent India was unfurled on the bank of the river Ravi, and all the delegates dipped in the cold water to solemnize the demand for complete freedom from colonial rule.

In the intervening years, the Hall had seen a lot of activity. In 1915, Lala Lajpat Rai, a leading Indian freedom fighter from Lahore, had established The National College inside Bradlaugh Hall. This was part of the Swadeshi movement to boycott, among other things, British-run educational institutes and provide quality education to Indians by Indian-run institutions. The College became a hotbed for anti-colonial activists, among whom the most famous was Bhagat Singh, who spent four years at this college. During this time, Bhagat Singh met many of his fellow revolutionaries, and in the adjoining Dwarka Dass Library (also established by Lajpat Rai), he read ferociously all types of literature, from manuals on Marxist revolution to the poetry of Keats!

Bhagat Singh was highly intelligent and well-read. He was a deep thinker, evident from the wide range of authors he quotes in his writings.

In April 1929, Bhagat Singh courted arrest after he and his associates exploded two firecrackers in the Central Legislative Assembly, New Delhi. He was charged with terrorism, and during the investigation, the police also found evidence implicating him in the earlier murder of a police officer in Lahore. In 1928, during a peaceful demonstration in Lahore against the Simon Commission, the police officer in charge ordered a baton charge. Lajpat Rai, leading the protest, was injured and later died in the hospital. According to the prosecution, Bhagat Singh and his associates planned and subsequently shot dead a police officer to avenge Rai. Bhagat Singh's trial drew widespread interest and criticism for how the British disregarded their own process for the provision of justice.

Bhagat Singh was convicted of what the British called the Second Lahore Conspiracy and sentenced to death. Whether he was guilty as charged of pumping four bullets into the victim is controversial. Although, for a part of his life, he did believe in violent revolution, it is doubtful if he could kill an unarmed man in cold blood. Even when the firecrackers, which the prosecution called bombs, were thrown in the Legislative Assembly, they were placed in a vacant area to avoid any injury, and the delegates were showered with leaflets, including some with the message, "It takes a loud noise to wake up the deaf."

Bhagat Singh was hanged on March 23, 1931; he was 23 years old. The site where the gallows were situated was subsequently demolished to make a busy road intersection named Shadman Chowk. Although there is no mention of Bhagat Singh in any Pakistani school or college curriculum, he has widespread support among a section of people in Lahore who have been demanding that the square be named Bhagat Singh Chowk. In 2012, the Lahore Municipal Corporation accepted this demand but then retracted as right-wing organizations erupted in protest. The case is still pending in Lahore High Court.

Manto and Lahore

Before the partition in 1947, Saadat Hasan Manto was happily settled in Bombay, a city he never stopped loving. However, he was not a stranger to Lahore. He had already been charged with writing obscene stories, and as that trial had taken place in Lahore High Court, he had travelled several times to attend the hearings. By coincidence, his friend writer Ismat Chughtai was also facing a trial on similar charges, and the two used to visit Lahore together, enjoying the shopping and food. Chughtai narrates that she, Manto, and Shahid Dehlavi, who had all been summoned by the court, had a whale of a time wandering in Lahore, shopping, and eating.

Once when they walked into a hotel, their mouths watered seeing hamburgers and hot dogs on the menu. Here, Shahid declared that they can't eat hamburgers as there is ham in them, but it is okay to eat hot dogs, which they did. Only two days later, they found out that there was no ham in hamburger, but there was pork in hot dogs. After knowing this, Shahid started retching till they got a mullah to advise that eating pork by mistake is not a sin. But the same night, Shahid and Manto got totally drunk and concluded that it is not possible to be sure what is in either and which one is halal and which haram, so it is best to avoid both and only eat tikkas!

Unfortunately, unlike the good fun Manto had in Lahore when he was on trial, his life when he permanently moved to Lahore post-partition was miserable and unhappy. For people like Manto who had a secular and non-religious view of the world, the partition of India along religious lines was a severe shock. Added to that was the atrocious and unbelievable violence they witnessed that caused unhealable trauma to their sensitive souls.

Manto spent the last seven years of his brief forty-three-year-long stay on this earth in Lahore, and they were not happy years. Still, it was in Lahore where he created arguably his best short stories and certainly his best works of non-fiction political satire, and it is Lahore where he rests in eternal sleep, still wondering (as per his self-written but omitted epitaph) who is the greater story writer, him or God?

After Manto arrived in Lahore via Karachi in January 1948, he spent the first six months in a state of shock. He had rejected the partition of India, but as he himself confessed in the end, he had to accept this monstrous reality (his words). Despite the acceptance, he found it difficult to understand what India is and what is Pakistan, a confusion he later penned in his masterpiece Toba Tek Singh. What he saw all around him sent him into despair, but as he writes, "I did not let myself be overwhelmed by despair. It was in that sea of blood that I plunged myself to come up with a few pearls of regret at what human beings had done to human beings." And when he finally managed to write short stories, the first one he wrote was Thanda Gosht (Cold Meat), but no one was prepared to publish it.

So, he wrote another one called Khol Do (Open it), which was published in Ahmad Nadeem Qasmi's Naqoosh and resulted in the magazine getting banned for six months. Much later, Thanda Gosht was also published in a special edition of the magazine Javed, resulting in the first post-independence obscenity trial for Manto.

While Manto wrote extensively on the hypocrisy, exploitation, and social evils that permeate our society, he was not and never claimed to be a reformer. There are no sermons in his writings, no judgments; he just writes how things happen and the way people behave in real-life situations. As he himself tells us, "The world should not make one understand; on the contrary, one should try and understand the world." And true to this in his stories, he leaves it to the reader to understand and decide what is good and what is bad.

It is well known that Manto was accused of writing obscenity and profanity. For this, he was charged and tried no less than six times - three times before and three times after Partition. Even though he was acquitted each time, for many, his stories were immoral and corrupting. Manto and his family lived in a flat in Lakshmi Mansion; in the same building lived the writer Mustansar Hasan Tarra. Tarrar later recalls how all youngsters were told by their parents to never ever read Manto's stories for they are dirty, and the result was that he had read all of them by the time he was 14!

While there is no doubt that some of Manto's stories have sexual content or contain language which can be considered objectionable for puritan folks, it is worth noting that of his 250 stories, only 20 or so are in this category. Yet as Manto himself points out with amusement that his critics ignore all his other stories and only read these few selected ones!

Manto's description of his fourth trial is as interesting to read as a short story itself. It is full of his keen observation and subtle humour as he exposes the corruption and unethical practice of the courts (everything needed wheels, otherwise, nothing would move). In narrating one incident where the honourable judge who seemed to take a dislike to him from the beginning admonished him for holding a packet of cigarettes in his hand, and then a few minutes later, the judge himself picked up a cigarette from his table and lit up, Manto illustrates the hypocrisy which is all too prevalent in our society.

Manto was charged under Section 292 of the PPC for publishing a story that was obscene and against public morality. His defense was based around the argument that the story "Thanda Gosht" (Cold Meat) was not obscene, whatever content it may have, because it is part of literature, and literature can only be good or bad but never obscene or immoral, as Oscar Wilde says, there is no such thing as a moral or an immoral book; a book is well written or badly written, that is all. The charges were initiated by Chaudry Mohammud Hussain, who was upset not just at the vulgar language and sexual content but also thought that the story portrays Muslims as so bay-ghayrat (without honor) that they let Sikhs rape even dead Muslim girls. He, like many others, failed to understand that the story tells us that even those who commit unspeakable acts of barbarity often have a little bit of humanity left in them, and somehow, sometimes this humanity finds a way to punish them. The defense produced a list of 32 witnesses to be called. The judge refused to let so many witnesses appear and only agreed on 14 but stopped after just seven had given their testimony. Among those who did appear were Faiz Ahmed Faiz and Sufi Ghulam Mustafa Tabassum; the prosecution produced four witnesses. Interestingly, Dr. MD Taseer, Faiz's hum zulf (brother-in-law), appeared for prosecution though from his statement it looks as if Dr. Taseer was more upset at the low literary quality of the story than at it being obscene. Agha Shorish Kashmeri also appeared for prosecution. After much deliberation and an agonizing wait, the judge found Manto guilty as charged and to everyone's surprise sentenced him to rather harsh 6 months' rigorous imprisonment and a fine of Rs 300.

In giving the reason for his decision, the judge stated that the standard of morality is not universal but specific to each area, and in Pakistan, the standard of morality to be followed is that which is in accordance with the Quran, and he feels that the story is obscene when the Quranic standards are applied.

An appeal was filed in the high court against the decision. When Manto and his lawyer saw the judge who was to hear the appeal, they were apprehensive as the judge had a long flowing beard and a dent on his forehead. However, to an even greater surprise, the judge gave a decision after just a single hearing, acquitting Manto of all charges and ordering that the fine he had paid be refunded to him.

While his stories are a masterpiece of Urdu literature, also well worth reading are Manto's non-fiction work, and paramount in this are his series of articles titled 'Letters to Uncle Sam.' Manto wrote a total of 9 such letters between 1951 and 1954. The letters are full of his laconic wit, sarcasm, and humour. Besides other things, they provide a commentary on the disastrous path Pakistan had started to follow.

In the first letter, Manto writes about his anguish at Partition and the fact that nothing much has changed for him:

"My name is Saadat Hasan Manto, and I was born in a place that is now in India. My mother is buried there. My father is buried there. My first-born is also resting in that bit of earth. However, that place is no longer my country. My country now is Pakistan, which I had only seen five or six times before as a British subject.

I used to be the All-India's Great Short Story Writer. Now I am Pakistan's Great Short Story Writer. Several collections of my stories have been published, and the people respect me. In undivided India, I was tried thrice; in Pakistan, so far, once. But then Pakistan is still young."

In another letter, he vents his scorn on the Mullahs and the USA:

"You have done many good deeds yourself and continue to do them. You decimated Hiroshima; you turned Nagasaki into smoke and dust, and you caused several thousand children to be born in Japan. Each to his own. All I want you to do is to dispatch me some dry cleaners. It is like this. Out there, many Mullah types after urinating pick up a stone and with one hand inside their untied shalwar, use the stone to absorb the after-drops of urine as they resume their walk. This they do in full public view. All I want is that the moment such a person appears, I should be able to pull out that atom bomb you will send me and lob it at the Mullah so that he turns into smoke along with the stone he was holding."

However, the most astonishing bits are those that show his insight and ability to see far into the future, and here in one of the letters, he writes: "India may grovel before you a million times, but you will definitely make a military aid pact with Pakistan because you are really worried about the integrity of this largest Islamic sultanate of the world, and why not, as our mullahs are the best antidote to Russia's communism. If the military aid starts flowing, you should begin by arming the mullahs and dispatch vintage American (dry cleaning) stones, vintage American rosaries, and vintage American prayer mats, with special attention to razors and scissors, and if you bless them with the miraculous prescription of vintage American hair dye as well then do understand that the cat is in the bag. The purpose of military aid, as far as I understand it, is to arm these mullahs. I'm your Pakistani nephew, but I am aware of all your machinations; but this heightened intelligence is all thanks to your politics (God save it from the evil eye). If this sect of mullahs is armed American style, then the Soviet Union will have to pick up its spittoon from here, even whose gargles are mixed up in communism and socialism." And incredibly, that is exactly what the Americans did in the 1980s, starting a process which has led to the destruction of Afghanistan and Pakistan.

In another of his articles, Manto tells us:

"These people who are commonly known as leaders, view politics and religion as that crippled, lame, and injured man, displaying whom our beggars normally beg for money. These so-called leaders go about carrying the carcasses of politics and religion on their shoulders, and to simple-minded people who are in the habit of accepting every word uttered to them in high-sounding vocabulary, they bandy about that they will breathe new life into this carcass. Religion is the same as it has always been and will always remain so. The religious spirit is a concrete reality which can never change. Religion is a rock which cannot be affected by even powerful waves of the sea. When these leaders cry their hearts out telling people that religion is in danger there's no reality to it. Religion is not something which can be endangered. If there is a danger, it is to these leaders who endanger religion to achieve their own ends."

How true this is, starting from Liaqat and his Objective Resolution to Zia and the present lot, a succession of leaders have used religion to get what they want and in the process have replaced the tolerant Pakistani society with militant jihadism that is causing so much misery to Pakistan and the world.

Despite his fame as a writer, the seven years Manto lived in Lahore were those of bare hand-to-mouth existence. In another of his letters to Uncle Sam, he says, "I am poor because my country is poor." While lack of opportunities and his alcoholism were major culprits, his generosity played a part as well. One of his friends recalls how he was walking along with Manto, who had just been paid Rs 20 for a story, when they saw a vendor selling gandaris dressed up as a groom. Manto went to him, gave him Rs 20, and said, "Go and attend to your wedding, I am buying all your stock." The financial problems had a disastrous effect on his relationship with his long-suffering wife Safia.

Not that he did not have opportunities to better himself by other means, for when he arrived in Pakistan, he saw all around him people, including his friends, scheming to grab abandoned houses and mills. They asked him to get something for himself, but he refused to take part in what he called loot and plunder. Some sources claim that Qudratullah Shahab allotted an ice factory to him, but the truth is that Shahab offered, and Manto's wife Safia was keen on it, but Manto refused to accept this.

One wonders why, faced with so many financial problems as well as hostility, he did not move back to Bombay. He would have been well aware of how well men like Sahir Ludhianvi are doing. The explanation for this is in another of his letters, "I want to live in Pakistan because I love this bit of earth, dust from which, incidentally, has lodged itself permanently in my lungs."

Writers are often asked the question for the motivation that makes them write, and in his article 'Why Do I Write', Manto states the reason he writes as simply because he has to eat and drink, and if he does not eat and drink, he cannot write. Here he laments that this is a sad fact of life, but that is how God has willed it, for while God tells us he is free of everything (bayniaz), Manto says this is wrong as He asks for prayer and prayer is like a buttered piece of bread God satisfies his appetite with.

As for Manto, eating was not that much of an issue. He hardly ate anything; a piece of bread dipped in curry was often what he had the whole day, it was the drinking which was a problem. Drinking excessive, cheap alcohol was what prematurely killed him.

The end was not pleasant, as recalled by one of his closest friends and neighbor in those days, Prof GM Asar. Manto's last story was "Kabootar Kabootri" that he read at a small FC College student gathering three days before his death. Days later, Asar Sahib was on his way to college when his youngest son told him that Apa Iqbal, Manto's sister, wanted to see him. When he went to the Manto home next door, he found her crying. When he asked her what is wrong, she replied, "Why are you asking me, go in and see your brother?" Prof Asar went into Manto's room and found him covered with a quilt. He called out his name but there was no reply, just a shudder in the heap. An ambulance was sent for that took Manto to Mayo Hospital. The doctor on duty felt for Manto's pulse and said casually, "You have brought him to the wrong place. You should have taken him to the graveyard. He is dead."

So, what drove Manto to drink himself to death? Like anything else, there are a multitude of factors. Mr. Shamim Ahmad, in his book "Torment and Creativity," has analyzed this in some detail. He considers the main cause for Manto taking up alcohol consumption in a society where this is considered amoral, and a sin was rebellion. This stemmed from Manto's resentment against a strict and puritan father who never showed any affection for his son from his second wife. Shamim Sahib also blames Manto's arrogance and oversensitivity at real and perceived insults from others leading to constant anxiety for which he used alcohol as a remedy. Added to this was the anxiety of making a living for himself and his family after he moved to Pakistan where there was no film industry and writing short stories was not very lucrative. While all these factors doubtless played a part, I think there were other reasons as well.

Manto, like many poets and prose writers, suffered from his sensitive nature; while the ability to feel the pain of others and to write about it so effectively creates beautiful literature, it also leaves the artist in the clutches of constant melancholy. And the events of 1947, the barbarity and depravity exhibited by humans during the riots, left deep wounds on his psyche from which he never recovered.

The final straw, which is not often mentioned, was the problems created by his honesty. Manto said things as he saw them; for him, the truth needed to be said openly regardless of who may get upset at this. Such people are often misfits in society, for when one speaks the truth openly, one is often left with few or no friends. Obviously, Manto was anti-Mullah and anti-religious orthodoxy, so it was natural that right-leaning writers and intellectuals shunned him - but what was worse was the so-called left-leaning intellectuals and liberals who were part of the Progressive Writers Movement, also disowned him! The reason for this was that Manto dealt in reality and not idealism, and while men like Faiz were able to survive due to their soft-spoken nature (although Faiz also stopped attending PWA meetings), Manto, with his quick temperament and saying things as they were bluntly, did not. One example of this is the way the Soviet Union was looked at by the progressive writers; they were all anti-imperialist and anti-USA, and so was Manto, but the difference was that the progressive writers looked at Soviet-style communism as a way to create the perfect society on earth. Manto suffered from no such illusions, and when many years later the reality of Soviet society and the suffering of its people became common knowledge, Manto's ability to look through the facade became all too clear.

The attack on his writings and him personally by those he considered his brothers in arms wounded him deeply, as he writes, "I was angry. What was wrong with these people, I asked myself. What kind of progressives were they who were only regressing? Why was this Big Red of theirs rushing headlong into black darkness?"

In the end, this rejection by everyone, as no one was prepared to hear the truth, led to his isolation and untimely death, which in a way could be considered a suicide. Manto dearly loved his three daughters, and the question is, how could he propel himself to an early grave knowing that he will leave them fatherless? And this thought was not alien to him, for he writes, "The fear that keeps gnawing at me is if I were to die suddenly, who will look after my wife and three minor daughters?"

Unfortunately, unlike romantic stories, as we see so many times in real life, love is not always enough for people to stay together or to keep on living. As one of his characters, Eshar Singh in "Thanda Gosht," says just before he cuts his own throat, "Man, mother begotten, is a strange thing."

Manto wrote his own epitaph, which he wanted to be on his gravestone:

"In the name of God, the Compassionate, the Merciful. Here lies Saadat Hassan Manto and with him lie buried all the secrets and mysteries of the art of storytelling... Under tons of earth, he rests, still wondering who among the two is the greater fiction writer: God or he."

His family decided not to put this on for obvious reasons, and a different text was used.

Manto lies buried in a rather obscure and forgotten plot in *Miani Sahib* graveyard. This is just what he would have wanted for he once wrote, "My melancholy heart trembles that one day this indecisive government will find itself pleased with me and place a medal on my coffin, which would be a great insult to my commitment to what I believe in." Unfortunately, Manto's fears did come true when in 2012 out of the blue the government decided to give him Sitara-a-Imtiaz, and once they had done this, they promptly forgot him again.

Unsung Hero

Pundit K. Santhanam is hardly remembered by anyone, yet directly or indirectly, he touched the lives of many and played an important role in India's independence. Born in Kumbakonam in 1885 to a high-caste Brahmin family and orphaned at an early age, Santhanam was sent by his elder brother, who was a successful lawyer, to England in 1906, where he studied at King's College, Cambridge. When he returned to Kumbakonam, he found out that since he had traveled over the sea, he was now excommunicated by his religion. Santhanam's family cut off all ties with him; even the brother who told him to go to England stopped talking to him! He could neither get a job nor a wife, and they did not forgive him even when he (later) died, as the priests refused to perform his last rites.

At this stage, Lala Lajpat Rai, known as the second lion of Punjab (the first being Ranjit Singh), whom he had met in England, invited him to come to Lahore, which in those days was much more religiously tolerant than most, perhaps all, parts of India. Within a few years, he became a leading lawyer of Lahore and even found himself a wife in 1916. Then in 1919, the Jallianwala Bagh massacre changed his life. Protests against the massacre and British oppression erupted all over Punjab, and Lahore was the center of this. The visionary entrepreneur Lala Harkishen Lal, who had set up the Punjab National Bank and other industries, was at the forefront of organizing the protests and was arrested for waging war against the king. Pandit Santhanam acted as the defense counsel for him and others charged free of cost.

In order to prevent the news about what they were doing from getting out of Punjab and igniting other parts of India, the British government had put in place a police cordon around the province, and no one was allowed to leave or enter. Pandit Santhanam decided to break the police cordon and smuggled himself out under the first-class berth of a railway compartment occupied by an Englishman. Reaching Shimla, he managed to meet and apprise Sir Sankaran Nair, a member of the Viceroy's Council, of the atrocities being committed under the guise of martial law, and it was thus that news of the black happenings in Punjab was leaked out to the nation, and the authorities had to act.

Later, when the Congress appointed a commission of inquiry into the Punjab atrocities consisting of Moti Lal Nehru, Fazlul Haq, C.R. Das, Abbas Tyabji, M.R. Jayakar, and M.K. Gandhi, Santhanam was designated its secretary and charged with the responsibility of preparing and publishing their findings. He completed his task in under a year. The report is a model of meticulous documentation (after interviewing 1,700 witnesses and recording evidence), and its publication was dubbed by Gandhi to be the "last nail in the coffin of the British Empire." Santhanam was jailed three times for offenses, which included participation in the Non-Cooperation Movement and satyagraha.

In 1920, Pandit Santhanam resigned his legal practice

during Mahatma Gandhi's Non-Cooperation Movement. The question was what to do for a living, and once again Lajpat Rai came up with an idea and suggested business. Thus, in 1924, Lakshmi Insurance Company (LIC) was born. And Santhanam, who by now was known as Pandit Ge, became the father of the insurance business in the Indian Subcontinent. LIC soon became extremely successful with branches all over India and even in East Africa. The company built huge official and residential buildings in many cities, including Lahore, Karachi, and Bombay.

Pandit G continued to lead the company and to play a role in politics, but the turn events took was what he did not want. In 1947, when his dream of Indian independence became reality, it was accompanied by the partition of Punjab. Tragically, at that time, he was in Kashmir with his family to escape the heat and dust of Lahore as he was suffering from an acute bout of asthma. He was never able to go back to his beloved Lahore, which had given him everything when his own flesh and blood had rejected him.

Migrating to Delhi, Pandit G could have got a post in Nehru's cabinet, but he was a heartbroken man. He decided to throw himself into helping the victims of the holocaust and became a member of the Advisory Committee to the Ministry of Relief and Rehabilitation, but he never recovered from the trauma of partition and died in 1949 at the age of 64.

There is an interesting end to this story: after the partition, many of the flats in the Lakshmi building in Lahore were allotted to migrants from India. Among them was the writer Sadat Hassan Manto, who wrote the most incredible yet disturbing stories about the partition. Manto lived and died in the Lakshmi Mansion in Lahore. So, in some way, though they never met, Pandit Santhanam and Sadat Hasan

Manto touched each other's lives, and Manto gave a voice to how Pandit Santhanam must have felt about the partition.

Ironically, one of them, a Hindu, never wanted to leave Lahore but had to, and the other, a Muslim had not intention to but, had to move to Lahore!

One of Lahore's greatest sons

Personally, I can't recall exactly when I became interested in Faiz Sahib's poetry. Like Faiz Sahib, both of my parents are from Sialkot. My maternal grandfather, a writer and scholar himself, was a devotee of Iqbal and Rumi. During my childhood, I had a lot of exposure to Iqbal's poetry, but I can't recall my grandfather ever quoting or mentioning Faiz, at least not as a poet, although they personally knew each other.

My only personal contact with Faiz Sahib's family was when I was a pre-med student at Sir Syed College Rawalpindi and owned a Yamaha motorbike. I used to visit a mechanic in Sadar Bazar where Mr. Shoaib Hashmi used to come as well with his Honda motorcycle, so I had a chance to chat with him a few times as we waited for our bikes to be tuned and serviced. For me, this was exciting as I was talking to a celebrity. However, Mr. Hashmi's celebrity status for me was not as the son-in-law of Faiz Sahib but as the brain behind the TV satire *Tal Matol* and the lucky man married to the beautiful Salima. We never discussed Faiz or his poetry.

Most likely, I became interested in Faiz Sahib during the

times of Zia martial law when his poems were used as a channel of protest and defiance against prevalent oppression. In particular, a 1985 performance by Iqbal Bano in Lahore clad in a black sari (Sari had just been banned by Zia as un-Islamic) caused those in the audience to become ecstatic as she declared:

> *Hum deekhain gay*
> *Woh din kay jiss ka waada hai*
> *Jab zulm o sitam kay koh a gra*
> *Roi key tarah urr jayeen gay*
> *Hum mehkoomo kay paon talay*
> *Jab dhartry dhar dhar dharkay gey*
> *Aur Ahlay Hakam kay sarr oopar*
> *Jab bijli kar kar karkay gey*

I was not fortunate to be among the audience, but I met some who were, and it made quite an impression on me. Since then, my interest in Faiz as a person and as a poet has kept on increasing with time.

No doubt, Faiz was a great Urdu poet, yet some critics may not agree and consider his poetry to be average or even mediocre. Well, that can be argued, but no one can argue that as a person, he was universally loved, even by his critics.

Faiz Sahib himself writes: "Our poets have always complained of the indifference suffered at the hands of their contemporaries; in fact, this has been a perennial theme in our poetry. As far as I am concerned, it is the other way around. I have had such kindness and love showered on me—by friends, acquaintances, and even virtual strangers—that I often feel that I do not deserve it. The little what I have done does not measure up to what I have received."

It is not hard to guess why he was thought worthy of so

much love, for Faiz Sahib always retained his humility and humbleness. He never retaliated when insulted and attacked. In all his works and writings, you will not see any bitterness towards those who criticized him, like when he wrote "Dagh Dagh Ujala" on the bloody birth of Pakistan or when in reply to everyone asking for a jingoistic patriotic song during the 1965 war he wrote "Spahey ka Merseya," an elegy for the thousands of young men from both sides of the border who died in a senseless war that achieved nothing. Each time he was crucified by so-called patriots, but he never retaliated. There is not even any resentment towards those who arrested him, sometimes without giving any reason, or forced him to leave his beloved city of light Lahore and Pakistan!

Faiz Sahib had a tranquil and calm nature but a sharp wit and sense of humor. TV actor Arshad Mahmood narrates that he once asked Faiz Sahib how come, despite that he has similar qualifications and attributes, yet has not achieved the same respect and acclimation. Faiz Sahib replied: "Bhae hum mein ur tum mein aik buniyadi farq hai (there is a basic difference between us)." Salman persisted, "Kya farq hai Faiz Sahib (what is that Faiz Sahib?" and Faiz Sahib replied: "Bhae humaray ustad Pitras Bukhari thay, aur tumharay Shoaib Hashmi (my teacher was Pirtas Bukhari and yours Shoaib Hashmi).''

In another incident, famous actress Shabana Azmi remembers a mushaira at the house of her father, poet Kaifi Azmi, who was a great friend of Faiz. Generally, Faiz Sahib was known as not good at reciting his own poetry, although if you listen to him, he has an individual style and grace. Anyway, an upstart poet at the mushaira said: "Kya khoob hoota kay Faiz Sahib jitna acha likhtay hai utna he acha sunatay bhee (how great it would have been if Faiz Sahib could recite his work as good as he has written it)." In his typical demure style, Faiz Sahib replied: "Bhae abb sub kuch hum hein karayen, kuch tum bhee tu karo na (Do I have to do everything, can't you do something)." Apparently, the poet did not open his mouth for the rest of the evening.

Faiz Sahib rejects art for art's sake and believes in striving through his poetry to bring about a change for the better in the condition of the poor and downtrodden people regardless of where they live, what language they speak, and what religion, if any, they follow.

Even his romantic poetry is not without this element. The poem 'Mujh say pehli see mohabbat' about which Faiz used to say is not his anymore as it now belongs to Madam Noor Jehan, is an example everyone is aware of where a poet who has just woken up to the realities of life explains why he is unable to offer the same love as before to his beloved.

Another of his beautiful poems is 'Raqeeb Say (To The Rival in Love)' also heavenly sung by Noor Jehan. In Urdu poetry, the rival for the beloved's affection is a loathsome subhuman character insulted at every opportunity. However, in typical Faiz style, he has only kindness and compassion for the man to whom he has lost his first love!

Tu ne Dekhi Hai Wo Peeshaani, Wo Ruskhsar,Wo Hont
Zindgi Jin Ke Tasawwur Main Luta Di Hum Ne
Tujh Pe Uthi Hain Wo Khoi Hui Saahar Aankhain
Tujh Ko Maaloom Hai Kiyoon Umr Gunwa Di Hum Ne

Till this point it is an example of a lover losing in love telling the victor how lucky he is and accepting it with good grace, but then there is a twist:

> Hum Pe Mushtarka Hain Ahsaan Gham E Ulfat Ke
> Itnay Ahsaan Ke Ginwaoon Tu Ginwaa Na Sakoon
> Hum Ne Iss Ishq Main Kya Khoya Hai,Kya Seekha Hai
> Juz Teray Aur Ko Samjhaoon Tu Samjha Na Sakoon

Somehow, Faiz suggests that the loser (himself) has also gained, but how is that possible?:
And Faiz Sahib explains:

> Aajzi Seekhi,Ghareebon Ki Himayat Seekhi
> Yaas O Harmaan Kay,Dukh Dard Kay Maani Seekhay
> Zer Daston Kay Musahib Ko Sumjhna Seekha
> Sard Ahon Kay,Rukhe Zard Kay Maani Seekhay

Once again Faiz Sahib has changed his defeat in love to something positive, something that makes him sensitive so he can feel the pain of the poor and helpless, he has expanded something personal to something universal. Such was his talent and passion.

And throughout his work, there is always hope. Hope for a better future no matter how bad things are and how dark the night is.

> Garr aaj tujh say juda hain tu kall baham hoon gay
> Yeh raat bhar key judai tu koi baat nehien
> Garr aaj aooj pay hai taalaye raqeeb tu kya
> Yeah chaar din key khudai tu koi baat nehien

Lahore was always in his heart and his soul especially when he was away for her due to being in jail or in exile. As he writes in his nostalgic poem dedicated to this city from exile.

> Sabza sabza sookh rahi hai, phiki zard dopahar

Deewaaron ko chaat rahaa hai tanhaai ka zahar
Door ufaq tak ghat-ti, badhti, utth-ti, girti rahti hai
Kohr ki soorat be-raunak dardon ki gandli lahar
Bastaa hai us kohr ke peeche roshnion ka shahar
Ae Roshnion ke shahar

Kaun kahe kis simt hai teri roshnion ki raah
Har jaanib be-noor khadi hai hijr ki shaharpanaah
Thak-kar har soo baith rahi hai shouk ki maand sipaah
Aaj mera dil fikr mein hai
Aye Roshnion kay shahar

Shabkhoon se munh pher na jaaye armaanon ki rau
Khair ho teri Lailaaon ki un sab se keh do
Aaj ki shab jab diye jalaayein, oonchi rakhein lau

Faiz Sahib was a man of many talents: poet, writer, editor, teacher, social worker, filmmaker, etc., but above all, he was a humanist, and his philosophy is eloquently paraphrased in his acceptance speech for the Lenin Peace Prize in 1962:

'Human ingenuity, science, and industry have made it possible to provide each one of us everything we need to be comfortable provided these boundless treasures of nature and production are not declared the property of a greedy few but are used for the benefit of all of humanity… However, this is only possible if the foundations of human society are based not on greed, exploitation, and ownership but on justice, equality, freedom, and the welfare of everyone… I believe that humanity, which has never been defeated by its enemies, will, after all, be successful; at long last, instead of wars, hatred, and cruelty, the foundation of humankind will rest on the message of the great Persian poet Hafez Shiraz: 'Every foundation you see is faulty, except that of Love, which is faultless....'

Agha Nasir, in his book 'Hum Jeetay Jee Masroof Rahay', which I would highly recommend to anyone interested in the context of Faiz Sahib's poetry, writes that Faiz Sahib considered his poetry as his Ishq and his social and humanitarian activities as his kaam. And to quote from one of his poems:

Woh loog bohat khush kismat thay
Jo ishq ko kaam samajtay thay
Ya kaam say ashiqi kertay thay
Hum jeetay jee musroof rahay
Kuch Ishq keeya, kuch kaam keeya
Kaam Ishq kay aaray aata raha
Aur kaam say Ishq ulajhta raha
Phir aakhir tang aa ker hum nay
Donoon ko adhura choor deeya

Blessed were those whose work was their devotion(Ishq)
While we lived we kept ourselves busy
Spent some time in devotion and some in work
Work kept hindering devotion
And they kept quarrelling with each other
So at the end getting tired of all this tussle
We left both the tasks unfinished

Well, Faiz Sahib, you may have left the world without finishing your work, and we are deprived of any more of your Ishq (I could not find an equivalent of Ishq in English), but the world no doubt is a better place because of you. God bless you, and may you rest in peace.

Raqs Zanjeer Pahen ker bhe kya jata hai (One can Dance in Chains as well!)

Neelo was one of the top actresses of Pakistani movies during the 60s and 70s. Renowned for her dance, she is the only Pakistani actress who made her cinema debut in a Hollywood movie (perhaps the only Pakistani actress who ever was in a Hollywood movie). This happened when in 1956, aged just 12 (but looking very grown up), she had a small role in the film Bhowani Junction, which was shot in and around Lahore. By the following year, Neelo was being cast in leading female roles.

As time went on, a budding romance developed between Neelo and screenwriter (later director) Riaz Shahid. Educated, dashing, and good-looking, Shahid had deep-seated liberal/socialist and anti-imperialist ideals. His movies reflected his beliefs and his sympathy with people who were struggling against imperial or foreign tyrannies. Shahid had met poet Habib Jalib at a pan shop near Evernew studios, and the two had become close friends. Jalib, of course, was and remains Pakistan's greatest ever revolutionary poet.

In 1965, the Shah of Iran came on a state visit to Pakistan. During his trip to Lahore, the governor of Punjab, the infamous Nawab of Kalabagh, arranged a semi-private musical evening for him. Neelo was asked to dance at the function. Shahid advised her not to, as he thought it was below the dignity of an artist to be summoned by a dictator to dance in front of a tyrant. Nawab of Kalabagh was the most ruthless goon of dictator Ayub Khan, so when Neelo refused to perform, armed men barged into her house and abducted her. She was threatened with jail, torture, and gang rape if she did not cooperate, and she was humiliatingly forced to agree to dance at the function.

What happened next is not clear. We know that she became unwell and had to be rushed to the hospital, where it was discovered that she had taken a large number of sleeping pills in an attempted suicide. One version of the story is that she collapsed during her dance, and another is that she actually became unconscious while being driven to the governor's house.

Either way, at the hospital, doctors washed out her stomach and saved her life. While she was recovering in the hospital, Riaz Shahid and Habib Jalib both visited her. It was during this visit that Riaz Shahid proposed to her, and soon they were married. Habib Jalib was inspired by this incident to write his famous poem:

Raqs Zanjeer Pehan Kar Bhi Kia Jata Hai..”
Tu Keh Na Waqif-E-Adab-e-Ghulami Hai Abhi,
Raqs Zanjeer Pehan Kar Bhi Kiya Jata Hai..
Aaj Qatil ki Yeh Marzi Kai Keh Sarkash Larki,
Sir-E-Maqtal Tujhay Korron Se Nachaya Jaey..
Mout Ka Raqs Zamanay Ko Dikhaya Jaey,
Is Tarah Zulm ko Nazrana Dia Ja Sakta hai..
"Raqs Zanjeer Pehan Kar Bhi Kia Jata Hai"
Dekh! Faryad Na Kar, Sir Na Jhuka, Paoon Utha,
Kal K Log Jo Karain Gey, Tu Abhi Se Kar Ja..

Nachtay Nachtay Azadi Ki Khatir Marr Ja!!!
Manzil-E-ISHQ Mein Marr Marr K Jiya Jata Hai..
"Raqs Zanjeer Pehan Kar Bhi Kia Jata Hai..."

In 1967, Riaz Shahid started to make the movie "Zarqa," which is the story of a female Palestinian freedom fighter named Zarqa. Shahid was eternally fascinated by Laila Khalid and had introduced variations of her character in his earlier movies. Zarqa is taken prisoner by the Israeli army, and to humiliate her, they make her dance in chains while they beat and torture her. Ijaz Durrani, once a husband of Madam Noor Jehan, actor, and part-time drug smuggler, sings on-screen, and the playback is by Mehdi Hasan. It was a slight modification of Jalib's poem.

Unfortunately, Riaz Shahid died of Leukemia in 1972, aged just 42.

To die a dog's death (kuttay key maut merna)

This is a popular catchphrase and curse in Urdu. It means to die a miserable death, alone, unloved, and unwanted. And sadly, many dogs as well as humans do die such a death in our part of the world.

Some of these humans are not just ordinary poor folks but highly talented individuals, one example is the poet, Saghar Siddiqui.

Even among sad stories, the tale of Saghar Siddiqui is exceptionally tragic. This exceptionally talented poet was from a well-to-do family of Ambala. When Pakistan came into being, he was 19 and already had made a mark as a poet. No one knows why and how he left everything including his family and migrated to Pakistan. Here like Manto, he refused to claim any property that had been left by those who had left for India. He became famous and admired as a poet but was unable to make any money from this. Out of his love for Pakistan, he wrote the national anthem for Pakistan which was rejected.

Soon he became disillusioned seeing the corruption and nepotism that was prospering day by day. His depression led to excessive drinking and then to morphine addiction.

When he could not afford to stay in cheap hotels, he started living on the footpath. He was thoroughly exploited by his friends who bought his poems which he continued to produce of exceptional quality, paying him peanuts and selling them under their names. No one knows how many poems and ghazals he wrote, many were lost as he burnt the paper on which he had written them to create a fire for heat in bitter winters. One of his famous writings is the lyrics to the dhamal "Lal Meri Pat" composed for the film "Jabroo" and used when this is performed at Sufi shrines in Sindh and Punjab.

In the last 5-6 years of his life, he was seen wandering around the circular road area in Lahore in a disheveled and malnourished state. One person recalls how one day he saw him like that while the radio was playing one of his ghazals. In those years, his constant companion was a stray dog he had befriended and with whom he shared the food shopkeepers would give to him.

It all came to an end when at the age of 46 he was found dead on the footpath with his dog sitting next to his body. It is said that the dog never left that spot and exactly one year after Saghar's death the dog was discovered dead one morning!

So Saghar literally died the proverbial dog's death, or maybe it was the dog that died Saghar's death!

Anyway, like many others, though destitute in life, Saghar was treated better by our dead-worshipping society, and he now has a mausoleum and is regarded as somewhat of a saint where people go to ask for their wishes to come true and give offerings and money, which of course is kept by those who are watching over the grave. So, the greedy bastards have not stopped exploiting even a dead Saghar to make money.

Zindigi Jabr musalsal key tarah kati hai
Janay kiss jurm key pai hai saza yaad nehien

Chandni Ratain (Moonlit Nights)

The moon has always had a mystic fascination that is not shared by the sun. Perhaps because we see the moon at night, and night itself is a time of mysteries, fear, and romance. Also, while we are assured that the sun will come out every day, the moon is more elusive. Some nights it may not appear, and then if it does, it can have a different size and shape every night.

Then, there are nights when we can see the full moon. In the past, this has been associated with some people turning into werewolves and some becoming mad (lunatics).

For poets who can imagine a full moon even during the daytime, such a night brings feelings of intense romance. And thus, so many poems and songs have been written about or inspired by the moon.

At the time of partition in 1947, when British India was partitioned, its film industry also got partitioned with artists having to opt for the new India or Pakistan. Noor Jehan was the top actress-singer of Bollywood in those days and migrated to Pakistan. Here, the center for the film industry was Lahore. In 1952, Syed Sibtain Fazli, an intellectual and visionary director, started to shoot the film "Dupata."

He had hired Syed Musheer Kazmi to write the lyrics, but the two of them got into an impasse regarding a certain song for one of the situations. Kazmi Sahib, who was making his debut as a lyric writer, wrote several versions of the song, but Fazli Sahib rejected all of them. As narrated by Kazmi Sahib himself, one night with no money in his pocket, he had to go to bed hungry. And there he was laying on his fragile charpai on the roof of a house where he rented a room, there was no prospect of sleep as he felt dejected and famished. It was a clear night; a full moon was shining, and the words came to him out of nowhere:

Chandni raatein Chandni raatein
Sab jag soye hum jaage
Taaro se kare baatein
Ho Chandni raatein Chandni raatein

In no time, the whole song was on the paper, and when the next day he took it to Fazli Sahib, he loved it, and thus was created what became one of the most famous songs sung by Madam Noor Jehan. The song helped to make "Dupata" the first super hit film made in post-partition Lahore. Although Feroze Nizami is credited as the music composer, in one of her later-day interviews, Noor Jehan claimed that Musheer Kazmi composed the tune as well.

Kazmi Sahib went on to become one of the most successful film and non-film songwriters. Among his creations is the famous patriotic song "Aye Rahe Haq Kay Shaheedo," which was adopted by the Pakistan Air Force and dedicated to the pilots who died during the wars.

Making Movies in Lahore

There is some optimism that after years of death-like slumber, the Pakistani film industry is undergoing a sort of revival. Even though at most 15 films are being produced in a year, looking back at the peak years when over 200 films were being produced, there is a long way to go.

In a way, the history of the Pakistani film industry reflects the history of the country. It was created out of nothing and at one time showed promise to become something good if not great, but then everything went wrong.

In pre-partition India, Lahore along with Calcutta was the major city for producing films outside Bombay. The pioneering Director/Producer of the Indian film industry, Himanshu Rai, and his stunningly beautiful actress wife, Devika Rani (who was the great-grandniece of Tagore), were both from Bengal. Yet it was Lahore where Rai made his first film called "The Light of Asia" in 1925. Later, the couple moved to Bombay to co-find the famous Bombay Talkies film production company, but some of their colleagues stayed in Lahore to develop the local film industry, earning it the name Lollywood.

The partition brought disaster to the industry. Like most businesses in Lahore, the film production studios were owned by Hindus who left for India while the frenzied mobs vandalized and burnt the buildings left behind. India Studio in *Baghbanpura a*nd Shori Studio on Multan Road became just burnt husks with only the walls standing.

Surprisingly, on the Upper Mall, the Pancholi Studios survived intact, even though its owner Diwan Sardari Lal came from a prominent Hindu family of Lahore. The reason given for this is that the keys of the studio were with a Muslim manager who confronted the mob when they came to burn it and shamed them into abandoning their plans.

Diwan Sardari Lal had stayed in Lahore, and the credit to make the first film for Pakistan goes to him. This was not an easy task since besides damage to infrastructure, many actors, directors, writers, musicians, and other human resources required to make a film had migrated to India.

The area that became West Pakistan used to provide the Bombay film industry with 25% of its revenue pre-partition and therefore it was a lucrative market for them. Dalip Kumar (Yousaf Khan) had already established himself as a leading actor in India, and he had sent his younger brother Nasir Khan to Lahore, buying him an office on McLeod Road to set up a film distribution company.

Nasir was also an actor, and Sardari Lal cast him as the hero of his film which was named "Teri Yaad." To play the female lead, he had Asha Posley, whose father Inyat Ali would be the music director.

Daud Chand was to be the director, but the choice of Qateel Shifai as the lyric writer was a surprise since he had no credentials as a lyric writer or even a poet, but what an excellent choice as he went on to become one of the greatest ever from the Sub-continent.

The film was completed in 3 months and released on Eid day, 7th of August 1948. It lasted only 5 weeks and was a flop. There were many reasons for this; it was released in a B-grade cinema Parbhat on McLeod Road as all the main cinemas were showing Bollywood movies. It was released at a time when the country was in the grip of depression due to the terminal illness of MA Jinnah (who died on 11th September) which did not help, but the main reason was that it was a very ordinary movie which was technically poorly made. Neither of the leading actors had much acting talent although Asha Posley was a very good singer.

Diwan Sardari Lal left for India in the early 1950s; however, despite the bleak scenario of the local industry, some continued to invest in it. One of them was Shaukat Hussain Rizvi who, along with his wife, the famous Noor Jehan, bought the burnt Shorey studio and rebuilt it quite literally as a lot of the restoration and decoration work was done by him by his own hands, it was renamed Shahnoor studios.

Financially, it was hard going, as one analyst describes, "They were bad days. Finance was shy. There were no established producers. Distributors were buying Indian films because there was a free import from India. Distributors were not even interested in buying Pakistani films, not to talk of financing them... There was great tension between India and Pakistan at that time and it was not uncommon to hear about an Indian attack or a financial collapse of Pakistan any day."

Importing Indian films was lucrative for many distributors who did not want the local industry to prosper. Not only had they managed to get almost free import of Indian films (the import duty was 2 paisa per foot while India charged Pakistan films 4 anas per foot) but they also used devious tricks. One of these was that they had hired a group of hoodlums who would go to any new Pakistani film released and as soon as the show started would shout, "*Daba, daba* (flop, flop)" causing disruption and forcing respectable families to leave the hall.

Many filmmakers simply copied already-made Indian films to produce "charbas."

The first locally made film which was a major success was "Qatil." Released in 1955 by GA Gul, it was directed by Anwar Kemal Pasha, whose father wrote the story. The songs were written by Qateel Shifai and were a major hit with the most famous being "Ulfat Key nai raho ko chala." And with the success of "Qatil" came the success of Qateel who never looked back. The financial bonanza allowed GA Gul to buy the Pancholi studios and make it the famous Evernew studios.

The local industry continued to expand with 32 films released in 1956, but it was only after the 1965 war broke out with India that the Golden age of the Pakistani film industry was ushered in as the screening of Indian films was completely banned. Soon the Pakistani cinema was giving its Indian rival a run for the money and called itself Lollywood with pride.

Alas, it did not last long; the first blow came from the loss of the Eastern Wing in 1977 and the talent which came from there.

On 18th March 1977, Nazar-us-Salam released the film "Aina," which became the most successful Pakistani film of all time. Running an unprecedented 48 weeks in the main cinemas and 401 weeks in all cinemas, it is the only Pakistan film to achieve the Crown Jubilee (Mega Hit), and with it, the Pakistan film industry reached the peak of its success.

In Urdu, we have a saying "nazar lag jana" meaning that when someone is doing too well or looking too good, someone's evil eye can bring them down and perhaps that is what happened. As if on cue on 21st April 1977, General Zia Ul Haq imposed martial law which lasted more than 10 years. During this time, Zia introduced strictly conservative Islamic Sharia laws and the film industry was subjected to oppressive censorship so much so that female actors were not allowed to appear with their heads bare and a man and woman could not be shown to be alone in a room even if they were supposed to be husband and wife. Along with this, VCRs from the Gulf arrived in the households and a flourishing trade in illegal Bollywood movies developed which people could watch at home without fear of Sharia or censors.

All this caused a rapid decline of the industry from which it is only just recovering. As mentioned before, the road to recovery is long and tortuous. A few years ago, after watching the Bollywood movie "Dangal," I asked Mazhar Zeidi (Producer Zinda Bhag) why Pakistan could not make such a movie, and he replied that it is technically impossible to do so in Pakistan. As an example, he told me that to become a good film editor, one needs to do a 2 or 3-year degree, but no one wants to spend so much time on this as everyone wants to be a producer or director.

Unfortunately, even for the films that are being made, the centre for film production is no longer Lahore (so no Lollywood), which was always Pakistan's intellectual and cultural heart but Karachi, and therefore sadly things will never be the same.

An appropriate mausoleum to Lahore's film industry is the dilapidated and abandoned building of Pakistan Talkies Cinema in the Walled City of Lahore. It was the first cinema of Lahore; in fact, the first for what later became Pakistan. It was opened in 1908 and at its peak used to seat 560 people. It closed in 2014.

Payar keya tu derna kya

In 1922, Syed Imtiaz Taj wrote a play titled "Anarkali," based on a tragic romance between a servant girl and a Mughal prince. This created the legend of Anarkali. Taj was from Lahore, and presumably, all the events in his play take place in Lahore, which at the time when this story unfolded, was the capital of the Mughal empire. The scenes of the play are staged in various parts of Lahore Fort.

Unfortunately, Taj never managed to get his play staged in Lahore, but the legend of Anarkali became permanently tethered to the city of Lahore where a tomb in her name is present and the entire shopping area around it, once the most sought after Bazaar of Lahore, is also called Anarkali Bazaar.

In the same year, 1922, a boy who was named Asif Karim was born. While his city of birth, Etawah in Uttar Pradesh, is recorded, what is not that well known is that he spent his childhood and teenage years in Lahore where his parents lived in Model Town. Without doubt, he would have heard about the legend of Anarkali during his time in Lahore, and he would have visited the Lahore fort where the story supposedly unfolded. Asif developed a great admiration for the Mughal emperor Akbar and a fascination for the story of Anarkali. He dreamed of making a mega movie based on this story with a slight change to present Akbar more positively.

In his early 20s, K Asif, as he now called himself, moved to Bombay like thousands of other men and women were doing in those days with hopes of being a part of the film industry. There he joined his uncle Nazir, who had also come from Lahore and is accepted as a pioneer of the Bombay film industry. Initially, K Asif worked as a tailor, but then he managed to have a break, and in 1945 he directed the film "Phool" which did moderately well. By this time, a film on the story of Anarkali had already been made by Ardeshir Irani in 1928. However, K Asif wanted to make a masterpiece on a scale much larger than that, in fact much larger than anything Bollywood had seen.

He managed to convince Producer Shiraz Ali Hakeem to back the project, and shooting for the film that was titled "Mughal-e-Azam" (The Greatest Mughal) started in 1944 with Chandra Mohan as Akbar. Mohan had recently played the roles of Jehangir (in "Shalimar") and Shah Jehan (in "Mumtaz Mahal") so looks like he was working on to play the role of all Mughal Emperors. Nargis was to play Anarkali, and DK Sapru was Prince Salim.

Unfortunately, when only 25% of the film had been completed in 1947, Hakeem left for Pakistan and the shooting stopped. In 1949, Chandra Mohan died, and the film shot so far was destroyed.

Not losing heart, Asif somehow met and convinced the construction magnate Shapoorji Mistry to invest in the project. This was no simple task as Shapoorji had no experience in making films, and to make a commitment for such an expensive venture must be credited to Asif's persuasiveness and eloquence of ideas.

The shooting of the film with a new cast that had Prithviraj Kapoor (Father of the Kapoor clan) as Akbar, Dilip Kumar (also born in 1922 and who was Asif's brother-in-law) as Prince Salim, and Madhubala as Anarkali started in 1951.

In those days, films with top stars were completed and released in 10-12 months and cost 1.2-1.5 million Rupees. Mughal-e-Azam was not released until August 1960 and involved over 500 days of actual shooting. It cost a staggering 15 million Rupees (adjusting for inflation this has been estimated to be between 500 and 900 million Rupees, making it the most expensive Bollywood film ever).

The film did very well commercially and critically and is still considered the most successful Bollywood film of all time.

The climax of the film is the dance sequence in the Shish Mahal (Palace of mirrors) where Anarkali sings the song "Pyar Kiya To Darna Kya" (When you love then why fear).

As I said, Imtiaz Taj wrote his play with Lahore Fort as the setting, and certainly, there is a Shish Mahal in Lahore fort where in his play the Nauroz function is celebrated and due to the mirrors, Akbar notices Salim exchanging amorous looks with Anarkali. Where the action takes place in the movie is not clear, for at the start of the film, Akbar's palace at Fatehpur Sikri is shown, and there is no mention during the film of Lahore, but we can assume that all the palace scenes in the film are taking place in 16th-century Lahore Fort.

K Asif himself got the idea of building the Shish Mahal after visiting Amber Fort in Jaipur. He decided to film a dance sequence in the Shish Mahal that would act as the climax of the film.

He asked his cinematographer RD Mathur if it was possible to film in such a set. Mathur said it would be hard, but yes, it can be done. As we know, the film was dragging on and constantly going over its budget as Asif refused to compromise on anything. This caused frequent arguments between Asif and Shapoorji, as Dilip Kumar tells us how Shapoorji would come to him agitated and would say, "*Eusaf zara Asif ko samjhao, kab tak film banayega, kya isay banate hue meray ga?*"

However, to his credit, Shapoorji always gave in and released the funds Asif wanted.

The set of Shish Mahal cost 1.5 million rupees. How to shoot the scene presented the biggest challenge for Mathur, as the hundreds of thousands of mirrors in the walls reflected the light from its source and thus made filming impossible. Mathur could not find a solution in any manual or from consulting with eminent experts like David Lean and Rossellini, who said it cannot be done.

But then he got the idea (which he says was from God) of using indirect light from reflectors. And so, in each shot, hundreds of reflectors were used to focus light on the target, and for each sequence, the reflectors had to be re-positioned, taking hours.

The song itself is a masterpiece. While Mughal-e-Azam was being made, Nandlal Jaswantla had released another film called Anarkali in 1953, starring Bina Rai. Asif had planned this song as a counter to the song "Mohabbat Mein Aise Kadam Dagmagaye" (also sung by Lata), but instead of a staggering defeated Anarkali, Asif wanted to present a defiant and proud Anarkali who has no chance of winning but it is the all-powerful emperor who looks scared of her.

Naushad Ali, one of the greatest ever music composers, made the tune using multiple classic ragas as the source. He rejected multiple drafts from Shakeel Badayuni for the lyrics till Naushad himself recalled a Poorbhi couplet from his childhood, *"Pyar kiya ka chori kari,"* and the rest of the song flowed from it.

A huge orchestra was used to create the music.

The song and the dance sequence have an iconic status among Bollywood songs. It is interesting that during the time the film was being made, Dilip Kumar and Madhuballa were having a real-life love affair which had hurdles due to their family members. Eventually, they broke up and even stopped talking to each other but as true professionals kept working on the film.

The sculptor KD Khedkar made a face mask of Madhubala as some of the more intense Kathak movements could not be done by her (she probably was already in the early stages of the heart problem that would lead to her untimely death) so the dancer Laxmi Narain did them wearing the mask, and shooting of vigorous dance segments were done from a distance.

When the shooting of the song was complete, K Asif got another brainstorm. As there was the scene where multiple reflections are whirling in the mirrors scaring the daylight out of Akbar, he now wanted a chorus, and Lata was asked to record a portion without music several times at various distances from the microphone. These were then mixed to create a haunting chorus from just one voice.

K Asif was 38 when the film was released and became arguably the greatest ever film of Bollywood history, curiously he never made another film and when he died in 1971 he left two incomplete films behind. I guess for Asif it was never about making a lot of movies but about making what one really loved in the way only a true lover wants to make it. In other words the lines from the song, '*Insan kissi say dunya mein ikk bar mohbat kerta hai, iss dard ko lay ker jeeta hai, is dard ko lay ker marta hai*' are appropriate to describe his professional life for after making his magnus opus he felt little incentive to make something else unless it was better which was almost impossible.

Anarkali Fact or Fiction

In the Southern part of Lahore's old city, there is a beautiful little mausoleum. It is a white stone building with eight corner turrets. Inside is a pure marble sarcophagus with one of the finest and elegant carvings anywhere in the world. The legend is that this is the final resting place of Anarkali, the tragic heroine of perhaps the most spectacular romance in history. Yet, was Anarkali a real person, or is she just a fragment of imagination? I am afraid this question is not easy to answer.

If we start our search for Anarkali from her tomb, we will see that along with the 99 names of Allah and two dates corresponding to 1599 and 1615 AD, there is carved in the inscription: "Ta qayamat shukr goyam kard gar khwish ra Ah! gar man baz beenam rui yar khwish ra" ("If could I behold the face of my beloved once more; I would give thanks unto my God till the day of resurrection") Majnun Salim Akbar (Totally Smitten Salim Akbar). It is possible to conclude that here lies Salim Akbar's beloved, and he is none other than the Mughal Prince Salim, son of Emperor Akbar and later the Emperor Jahangir.

However, it is not as simple as that. Before we start

looking at the historical evidence for the existence of Anarkali, let us remind ourselves of the story. Well, actually, there are several rather different versions of the story. The most popular is the one used in the most spectacular of the several Anarkali films made over the years, "Mughal-e-Azam" (1960), starring Dilip Kumar and Madhubala. Emperor Akbar (Prithviraj Kapoor) and his Rajput wife, Jodha Bai (Durga Khote), pray for a son. The news of their prayer being answered is brought to the emperor by a maid. The overjoyed Emperor gifts his ring to the maid and promises to grant her any one wish she asks. The son, Prince Salim, grows to be a weak and pleasure-loving boy. His father sends him off to war in order to teach him courage and discipline. After 14 years, Salim returns as a distinguished soldier (Dilip Kumar). Salim falls in love with Anarkali (Madhubala), a court dancer. Salim wants to marry Anarkali, and they have secret meetings. However, the jealous Bahaar (Nigar Sultana), a dancer of a higher rank, wants the crown of India, and she attempts to make the prince love her so that she may ascend to queenship. Being unsuccessful in her venture, she vents her disappointment by exposing the love between Salim and Anarkali. Salim pleads for Anarkali's hand, but his father says, 'Yeah Shadi Nehien Ho sakti (This wedding cannot happen)' and throws Anarkali into prison.

Despite imprisonment, Anarkali refuses to reject Salim. Salim rebels and amasses his own army to confront Akbar. Salim is defeated in battle and is sentenced to death by his own father but is told that the sentence will be revoked if Anarkali, now in hiding, is handed over to face death in his place. Akbar's subjects plead for the emperor to spare his son, and Anarkali comes out of hiding to save the prince's life. She is condemned to death and will be entombed alive.

Before her sentence is carried out, she pleads to have a few hours with Salim as his make-believe wife. She is granted the wish, as she agrees to drug him afterwards so that he cannot interfere with her entombment. As she is being walled up, Akbar it is disclosed that the maid to whom Akbar gave his ring and the promise to grant any which is none other but Anarkali's mother!

Anarkali's mother takes advantage of this and begs for her daughter's life. The emperor relents and arranges for Anarkali's secret escape with her mother into exile. He stipulates, though, that they are to live in total obscurity, and that Salim is never to know that Anarkali still lives.

If the above is true, then who built the tomb? Possibly when Salim became the emperor, he resumed his affair with Anarkali and built the tomb when she died. As Emperor Jehangir, Salim wrote a chronicle called "Tuzaq a Jehangiri" that covers the period from the time he acceded to the throne in 1605 to 1622, but there is no mention of Anarkali in this at all! So if the emperor had married her or even had her as his consort, why did he not write about it in his memoirs? Similarly, in his memoirs, Akbar does not mention Anarkali, nor does she appear in the writings of any historian of that time.

From the dates on the sarcophagus, it is assumed that 1599 is the date of death for whoever is buried there and 1615 is when the tomb was built, which indeed was during Jehangir's reign. So once again, if he had built such an exquisite structure, why not record it in his diary?

In another version of the story, Anarkali was a *bandi* (slave girl) of Akbar and his favorite concubine. One day while sitting in the house of mirrors, Akbar notices Anarkali and Salim exchanging smiles, deducing that they are having an affair, he orders Anarkali to be buried alive, and in this version, this is what happens. This ending was used in the 1953 film "Anarkali," starring Pardeep Kumar and Bina Rai, where Anarkali sings the song "Yeah Zindagi Ussi Key Hai" while being entombed and Salim is trying to save her but fails, managing to bang his head on the tomb and weep.

The first historical mention of Anarkali is found in the travelogue of a British tourist and trader, William Finch. Is it possible that this is another conspiracy of the Farangis to scandalize Indian and Muslim royals? We don't know. What we know is that writing around 1612, Finch narrates that Anarkali was one of the wives of Emperor Akbar and the mother of his son Danial Shah. Akbar developed suspicions that Anarkali had relations with Prince Saleem (Jahangir). What the great emperor cuckolded by his own son, he will be the laughingstock of the empire if anyone found out and thus he ordered the girl to be buried alive in a wall of Lahore Fort. Jahangir, after ascending the throne, had a splendid tomb constructed, at the present site, in memory of his beloved.

Basing his analysis on the above account, Abraham Eraly, the author of "The Last Spring: The Lives and Times of the Great Mughals," suspects that there "seems to have been an Oedipal conflict between Akbar and Salim. He also considers it probable that the legendary Anarkali was nobody other than the mother of Prince Daniyal." Eraly supports his hypothesis by quoting an incident recorded by Abul Fazl, the court historian of Akbar. According to the historian, Salim was beaten up one evening by guards of the royal harem of Akbar. The story is that a madman had wandered into Akbar's harem because of the carelessness of the guards. Abul Fazl writes that Salim caught the man but was himself mistaken to be the intruder. The emperor arrived upon the scene and was about to strike with his sword when he recognized Salim. Most probably, the intruder was Prince Salim who went to the Royal Harem where no man except the Emperor was allowed, and when he got caught, the story of the madman was concocted to put a veil on the indecency of the Prince.

But the accounts of the British travelers and consequently the presumption of Eraly are falsified when one comes to know that the mother of Prince Daniyal had died in 1596, which does not match the dates inscribed on the sarcophagus.

As regards native Indian writers, Anarkali first makes an appearance in Noor Ahmed Chishti's book "Tehqiqaat-i-Chishtia" (1860). He writes, "Anarkali was a beautiful and favorite concubine of Akbar the Great, and her real name was Nadira Begum or Sharf-un-Nissa. When she died of natural causes or being poisoned by other jealous harem ladies, Akbar ordered to create this grand tomb."

Syed Abdul Lateef, in his book "Tareekh-i-Lahore" (1892), agrees that Anarkali's actual name was Nadira Begum or Sharf-un-Nisa, and she was one of Akbar's concubines. He suspected illegitimate relations between Prince Saleem and Anarkali and, therefore, ordered that Anarkali be buried alive in a wall, and the tomb was later built there by Jahangir (Saleem) when he succeeded to the throne.

In his compilation, titled "Tareekh-i-Lahore" (1897), Kanhaya Laal writes that Nadira was a beautiful concubine in the court of Akbar and was endowed with the name Anarkali on the basis of her pink complexion and ravishing beauty. He also opines that she died a natural death when Akbar was on a tour of Deccan. Later on, Akbar got this graceful tomb built.

Abdullah Chagatai, an 18th-century historian and architect, has given a very different version. He claims that the tomb, basically built in the center of a pomegrante garden, contains the grave of Jahangir's wife Saheb Jamal, who was very dear to him. With the passage of time, the lady's name disappeared into oblivion, and the tomb was christened by the people as the tomb of Anarkali on the basis of the surrounding pomegranate gardens.

Another scholar, Muhammad Baqir, the author of "Lahore Past and Present," is of the opinion that Anarkali was originally the name of the garden in which the tomb was situated, but with the passage of time, the tomb itself came to be named as that of Anarkali's. This garden is mentioned by Dara Shikoh, the grandson of Jahangir, in his work "Sakinat al-Auliya," as one of the places where the Saint Hazrat Mian Mir used to sit. Dara also mentions the existence of a tomb in the garden, but he does not give it any name.

Muhammad Baqir believes that the so-called tomb of Anarkali actually belongs to the lady named or entitled Sahib-i Jamal, another wife of Salim.

Noted art historian R. Nath argues that there is no wife of Jahangir on record bearing the name or title of Anarkali to whom the emperor could have built a tomb and dedicated a couplet with a suffix Majnun. He considers it absolutely improbable that the grand Mughal emperor would address his married wife as 'yar' and designate himself as 'majnun' and aspire to see her face once again. Seems possible considering that Jahangir was a prolific mongrel with over 800 wives and concubines in his harem.

In another version, Salim actually managed to get Anarkali away from the clutches of Akbar and kept her hidden in Kasur near Lahore, and when he became emperor, he married her and gave her the title of Noor Jehan, his favorite wife. This is highly unlikely since Noor Jehan has some history before she married Jahangir and the marriage did not happen till 1611 while Salim had been the head honcho since 1605.

Anarkali's story has certainly fired the imagination of drama writers. The trend started when Syad Imtiaz Taj wrote and organized a stage drama of this story in 1922, Taj said that he had taken inspiration from the story from folk songs, and it is a work of fiction. Unfortunately, the drama was never staged in Lahore.

The first film based on the story was released in 1936 and it was followed by the post-partition Indian film "Anarkali" in 1953 starring Pardip Kumar and Bina Rai. This contains some of the most beautiful songs by Lata including 'Yeah Zindigi Usi key hai' and 'Aja abb tu aaja'. Interestingly, Pakistani Diva Noor Jehan had a role in this movie as Noor Jehan, although I am not sure in what context Jehangir's future wife appears in Anarkali's love story, however, Noor Jehan certainly had a major role in the 1958 Pakistani production of Anarkali where she played the role of Anarkali and also sang some of the most beautiful songs like *'Sada hoon apnay pyar key' and 'jaltay hain arman meera dill roota hai'*. I have already mentioned "Mughal-e-Azam" which was the most expensive and commercially the most successful of the Anarkali films and also had the most acclaimed soundtrack with the song *'Jab pyar kya tu derna kya'* becoming a cliché for all times.

So, is Anarkali just a myth? Possible but there is documented history that around 1599 Akbar and his favorite son Salim did develop some serious issues. Salim did raise the banner of rebellion against his father but most historians think that the reason was him getting frustrated of waiting, that reminds me of our poor price Charles!

The learned Lahore scholar Anna Suvorova thinks that

the legend of Anarkali is part of the legends of immured brides and girls that are associated with many cities and buildings of the world. She details more than 20 examples from Scotland to Azerbaijan of a young woman or a female child who was sacrificed by being immured alive in the foundation or structure of a castle, temple, tower, or even a bridge to make it strong and everlasting. Why a female? Well, because the human sacrifice has to be pure, and a virgin female can be verified as pure while there is no such chance to confirm the virginity and purity of a male. Therefore, Suvorova suggests that the legend of Anarkali developed around the tomb of some unknown person (who may be a man) to satisfy the need of an immured female for the Mughal fort in Lahore.

Anyway, unfortunately, the mystery of Anarkali may never be solved. As for my favorite song from Anarkali films, it is Noor Jehan's *'Sada hoon apnay pyar key,'* which beats Lata's *'Yeah Zindigi Ussi key hai'* by a narrow margin just because it is so poignant and haunting. Noor Jehan was born in Kasur where according to one of the legends, Anarkali spent her life in hiding. Is it possible that a part of her spirit influenced Noor Jehan when she sang this song? Is it possible this is the reason why she prophesies when she tells us: *'Kissi say jo na khul sakay woh zindigi ka raaz hoo'* (I am a mystery of life that no one can solve)? I leave it for you to decide.

Jews of Lahore

Off Zafar Ali Road in Lahore is situated Sanjan Nagar Institute of Philosophy and Arts. Given the restrictions in Pakistan on such activities, how much philosophy and art is created there, I do not know, but the building that houses this non-profit organization has a fascinating past.

When the Nazis came to power in Germany, conditions for the Jews started to get worse day by day. Many of them started to leave Germany and move to other parts of the world. Hermann Selzer and Kate Neumann were two such young Jewish students who wanted to study medicine. As admission to medical schools was closed for Jews, they moved to Rome where Jews were still allowed to study medicine. The two had briefly met in Berlin previously, and now in Rome, they fell in love and got married in 1935.

Europe was fast becoming a dangerous place for Jews. Many were leaving and settling in Palestine, where the Selzers thought of moving as well. But then at a dinner party, they met an Italian businessman who had traveled in India, and he said, "Why are you thinking of going to Palestine? You're young, you're cosmopolitan, you have medical degrees; in India they need European doctors. Go and have a look at India."

Hermann Selzer then toured various cities of India, including Delhi and Bombay, but for some reason decided to settle in Lahore. I am not sure why he chose Lahore, but my guess is that he got good vibes from a city known for its tolerant and welcoming nature for newcomers.

So, they moved to Lahore where in 1939, their daughter Hazel was born. They set up a successful medical practice, and one of the premises where their residence and clinic was is now the building used for Sanjan Nagar Institute of Philosophy and Arts!

They loved Lahore, and the people of Lahore welcomed them with open arms and loved them back despite the fact that there were hardly any other Jews in the city as the majority of the 2000 or so Indian Jews lived in Karachi or Bombay.

Unfortunately, during the war years, as Poland had canceled citizenship for people like the Selzers, they were considered stateless and interned in camps created for enemy aliens along with Nazi sympathizers!

After the war was over, they resumed their life in Lahore. The creation of Pakistan in 1947 did not change anything for them, and they continued to be accepted in Lahore, which was now part of Pakistan. The Selzers intended to spend their entire life in Pakistan, but things changed due to the Arab-Israeli conflict, which made people in Islamic countries, including Pakistan, increasingly hostile towards the Jews. Being Jewish was no longer just being Jewish; it was being Zionist. An incident when Dr. Kate Selzer's car was surrounded by an angry mob convinced them that they had to leave Pakistan.

So, in 1971, with heavy hearts, they left their beloved Lahore and moved to Israel. Their daughter, Hazel, and son,

Michael, had a deep attachment to Lahore and the two houses they had lived in. Initially, this house was 55 Lawrance Road, and later the Selzers moved to Gulberg. Hazel and Michael spent their childhood in boarding schools; for a few years, this was in India, but then for much longer, it was in England. During all this time, they constantly waited for the holidays when they would go back to Lahore to see their parents and the house they loved.

Hazel Selzer, now called Hazel Kahan and a PhD in Psychology, never forgot Lahore, which she calls the Magical city. She writes, "My home in Lahore, even my room, was very special to me. Whenever I was away [to boarding school and later on], I always thought about that house. Since the house was in Lahore, the city also took on some magic for me."

Then, in 2011, after 40 years, she came back to Lahore, managing to revisit the home of her childhood (which now belongs to a powerful political family of Pakistan) as well as the second house of her teenage and early adult years. Following this visit, she started a blog on Lahore and spoke about it on radio and television.

In 2020, she put together her experiences in a book called 'A House in Lahore: Growing up Jewish in Pakistan'. In this book, she describes the sadness and trauma of repeatedly leaving Lahore and her parents to go to boarding schools, which she and her brother dreaded. Their parents convinced them that this was so they could get the best education. Later, she figured out that this was because her parents were worried that their children might leave Judaism. And no, the fear was not that they would convert to Islam but to Catholicism!

It is sad that a city which was known for its tolerant and accepting atmosphere, for the friendliness and good nature of its inhabitants, not only in India but even far away, has become so intolerant over the years that even local people have to watch what they say.

Perhaps the cause for this metamorphosis is what another Lahore lover who was forced to leave Amrita Pretam suggested:

Kisey Nain Panjaan Paaniyan Wich
Diti Zahar Rala,
Tey Unhan Paniyaan Dharati Nuu
Dita Paani Laa

Someone has mixed poison
in the five rivers' flow
Their deadly water is, now,
irrigating our lands galore

Ps: it must be mentioned that Hazel Kahan as she is known now has only experienced warmth and hospitality from Lahoris during her visits.

The Legend of Dulla Bhatti

Among many others buried in the Miani Sahib Graveyard is the eternal resting place of Dullah Bhatti, and this name is recited repeatedly wherever in Punjab the *Lohri* Festival is celebrated. Although originally from the Himalayas region and signifying the end of the short days of winter, Punjab folklore links Lohri to the tale of Dulla Bhatti, and this is a central theme of many Lohri songs.

Dulla Bhatti, whose real name was Abdullah Bhatti, lived in Punjab during the reign of Mughal Emperor Akbar. In those days, Mughal officials patronized the practice of selling girls from Punjab in slave markets, and Dullah Bhatti used to rescue these girls regardless of their religion and caste. He also took up arms to protect poor peasants of all religions and castes from rapacious Imperial tax collectors. Thus, Bhatti is to Punjab what Robin Hood is to Sherwood Forest or what William Tell is to Switzerland. Bhatti was hanged in Lahore in 1599.

Among those he saved were two Hindu girls Sundri & Mundri, whose names gradually became a theme of Punjab's folklore. As a part of Lohri celebrations, children go around homes singing the traditional folk songs of Lohri with the name "Dulla Bhatti" included. One person sings, while others end each line with a loud "Ho!" sung in unison. After the song ends, the adult of the home is expected to give snacks and money to the singing troupe of youngsters, a bit like trick or treat.

Bhatti was a Muslim, and in 1947, East Punjab was ethnically cleansed of all Muslims, but curiously, the heroism of Bhatti is now only celebrated in East Punjab, while Muslim West Punjab has abandoned this festival.

The Other Amrita

Punjabi poetess Amrita Pritam is very well-known. A beautiful woman who wrote enchanting poetry and believed in humanity to be above religion, caste, or creed. However, there is another Amrita who is not that well known but was in many ways like her, beautiful, talented, and a free thinker ahead of her time. In fact, this other Amrita was a lot more adventurous in her life.

In 1912, Bamba Duleep Singh, the granddaughter of Maharaja Ranjit Singh, was finally given the permission to visit India. She advertised in the newspaper for an appropriate companion; the lady selected was Marie Antoinette Gottesmann, who was a well-known Hungarian opera singer and belonged to a Jewish aristocratic family. While in India, Marie Antoinette met and fell in love with Umrao Singh Sher-Gil Majithia, a Sikh aristocrat and a scholar in Sanskrit and Persian. (Looks like finding husbands was one of the aims of the visit as Princess Bamba also married an English doctor living in Lahore.)

Amrita Sher-Gil was born in 1913, the year when Rabindranath Tagore became the first Indian, in fact, the first Asian to win the Nobel Prize. She spent her childhood in

Shimla. Unfortunately, Marie Antoinette discovered that she had miscalculated thinking Sher-Gil was rich, but he was not, and the family always had financial trouble.

Amrita started painting and drawing from an early age, and when only 11, her mother took her to Italy to study at an art school. In less than one year, the precocious child was expelled for her insistence on drawing nudes. In 1929, Amrita was enrolled in another art school in Paris and spent 5 years there. Her paintings were being praised to be a lot more mature than her age, and she had a promising career ahead of her.

Despite the opposition from her mother and father, she decided to move back to India. In her own words, she recalled years later, "As soon as I put my foot on Indian soil, my painting underwent a change not only in subject and spirit but in technical expression, becoming more fundamentally Indian. I realized my artistic mission then: to interpret the life of Indians and particularly of the poor Indians pictorially, to paint the silent images of infinite submission and patience, to depict the angular brown bodies, strangely beautiful in their ugliness, to reproduce on canvas the impression their sad eyes created on me." Amrita was able to fuse Western and Eastern art and create her own style.

Although strongly influenced by Rabindranath Tagore and the Bengal School of Arts, Amrita, even at such a young age, was a true revolutionary. She criticized other artists from India for being too timid with color and created art with a flamboyant and bold use of colors.

And she was no less bold and adventurous in her personal life, with a string of affairs with both men and women that she shares through her letters without any embarrassment. She lived her life as few women of her time dared to, even in Europe, let alone India.

Interestingly, she was a good friend of Pandit Nehru but never made his portrait. When someone asked why, she replied, "Because he is too good-looking!" Sadly, she never found recognition as an artist during her time, although her lifestyle caused many tongues to wag. Perhaps some of these were the sour grapes type, like Khushwant Singh, who goes a bit too far trying to paint her as a sex-mad nymphomaniac.

It is possible that in due course she would have established herself, but an untimely death at the age of 28 (cause not known) ended this possibility. Since then, she has received wide recognition in India and internationally, with her work often highlighting the plight of women, acting as a beacon for feminist movements. Her paintings have fetched some of the highest prices paid for a painter from India.

It is worth noting that it was Lahore where the only solo exhibition of her work took place in 1937. It was Lahore where she decided to settle, died, and was cremated in 1941 (the same year as Tagore). Alas, Lahore and Pakistan do not give her any recognition.

When in the 1990s Feroz Abbas Khan decided to create a play (which is an adaptation of A. R. Gurney's American Play Love Letters) in the Indian context, he based the central character on Amrita Sher-Gil, not Amrita Pritam as some mistakenly believe. Titled Tumhari Amrita, it had Shabana Azmi playing Amrita and was a big hit in India, the US, and Pakistan (yes, it was staged in Pakistan, something unthinkable now).

Kabhi Kabhi

Yash Chopra, who passed away in 2012, is arguably the most successful producer-director in Bollywood history. I am sure Yash would acknowledge that the poet Sahir Ludhianvi played a major part in his success story. There was an 11-year age difference between Yash (born 1932) and Sahir, however, both came from Punjab. Yash was born in Lahore and lived there till 1945; by that time, Sahir, who was also living in Lahore, had published his collection of poetry called "Talkhian" and had established himself as a poet. Yash lived at the home of his brother BR Chopra, who was a film journalist. Educated in Lahore, BR was 18 years older than Yash, so more of a father to him. After the 1947 partition, Yash for a while lived in Ludhiana, the birth town of Sahir, and then moved to Bombay to try his luck in the film industry.

By that time, BR Chopra had already established his film company and was hobnobbing with stars. To impress his younger brother, he asked him which celebrity he would like to meet, thinking the young man would ask for a young and pretty starlet. However, without hesitation, Yash replied Sahir Ludhianvi. Yash had been reading Sahir's poetry since it had been published. After their first meeting at BR's house, the two gradually developed a firm friendship that lasted a lifetime.

Sahir had arrived back in Bombay from Lahore in 1949, and after 2 years of struggle, had become a successful lyric writer with the movie "Naujawan" released in 1951. He had not yet worked for BR Chopra and was also having problems keeping on good terms with the big-shot music directors of Bombay. In 1957, when BR started production of his film "Naya Daur" (a new era), Yash, who was working as an assistant with him, played an instrumental role in getting his favourite poet the job of lyric writer. The film that promoted the vision and optimism of Nehruvian India was a big hit. The same year, Sahir had a major success with Guru Dutt's "Pyaasa," but by the end of the year, both SD Burman and OP Nayyar had refused to work on any more films with Sahir.

The Chopra brothers decided to stay firmly behind Sahir. Part of this was (as Yash many years later said in an interview) the Punjabi connection, but more importantly, they could see the immense talent Sahir had, which could bring success to their films.

And so, Sahir continued to work for BR Films and wrote many memorable songs. So much did the Chopras value Sahir that, knowing his fear of heights (Sahir never flew in an aircraft in his life except once), if they were thinking of hiring a music producer and found out he lived in a flat on a high level, they would drop the idea!

In 1971, Yash left the firm of his brother and started his own film production company, Yash Raj Films. Sahir was one of the few who followed him and told him, "Do not pay me anything upfront. If your film is successful and you can afford to pay me, do it then."

Lucky for Yash, his first film, Daagh, was a superhit with songs penned by Sahir. Daagh was followed by several commercially successful but musically ordinary films by Yash Chopra. As the emphasis was now on action and beat, Sahir's poetry had to take a back seat. To keep his friend happy, Sahir agreed (with some reluctance) to write songs like "Gapche Gapche Gum Gum" etc.

And then came Kabhi Kabhi. Yash Chopra had read the poem Kabhi Kabhi from Sahir's first collection of poetry well before he met Sahir. In 1975, he decided to make the movie Kabhi Kabh based loosely on the life of Shair. As the title was Kabhi Kabhi, the title song was to be the same, and hence Sahir wrote the lyrics for this song. Some people mistakenly think that the poem and the song have the same words. The fact is that the film song Kabhi Kabhi is completely different from the poem Kabhi Kabhi. Not just in words but also in sentiments. The poem is one of total loss, about love unfulfilled and echoes thoughts of a poet who has nothing but regrets. Perhaps it was written when Sahir had accepted his love affair with Amrita was doomed. It also in parts reminds us of Faiz's "Aur bhe ghum hain zamanay mein" in that it demonstrates the contrast between romantic fantasy and stark reality. On the other hand, the song by Lata and Mukesh are the words of a lover who has achieved his desire, but only in a dream while in reality, his love belongs to someone else though he still likes to keep believing that she is his forever. In simple terms, both songs express the feelings of a failed lover, one in a reality where he has accepted defeat and is waiting for death and one in a fantasy where he has created an alternate reality for himself. And although the song became a massive hit, the words of the poem more accurately describe how Sahir must have felt during the few years he lived after the film was released. The film also featured what can be considered Sahir's swan song in "Main Pal do Pal ka Shayar hoon."

Sahir worked in one more film for Yash, Kala Pathar. But when Yash Chopra wanted to start his next project, Sahir was no more in this world. He convinced Javed Akhtar, who so far had been a script and dialogue writer, to become a lyricist for the film Silsila.

First Pakistani National Anthem and a poet from Lahore

The Pakistani national anthem has had its fair share of controversies. The first is the claim that it is in Persian and not Urdu.

The second controversy about the anthem is even more intriguing. It is claimed that the founder of Pakistan, MA Jinnah, commissioned a Hindu poet to write Pakistan's national anthem.

Jagan Nath Azad kicked it off when he wrote in his book "Hayat-e-Mehroom" (published 1987): "I was still in Lahore, living in my house in Ramnagar with the intention of never leaving Lahore. In those days, Pakistan probably had only two radio stations: one in Lahore and the other in Peshawar. When Radio Pakistan (Lahore) made the announcement of the founding of Pakistan that night, it was followed by a broadcast of my National Anthem *'Zarre tere hein aaj sitaaron se taabnaak, Ai sarzameen-e-Pak'*. The other side of this image is that on the next day, 15 August 1947 – when India was celebrating its independence – Hafeez Jalandhari's anthem 'Ai watan, Ai India, Ai Bharat, Ai Hindustan' was broadcast by All India Radio (Delhi)."

Then in 1993, Indian scholar Dr. Khaliq Anjum, writing his foreword to a book on Azad Sahib, wrote, "Not many people know that, while still in the land of his birth, Azad sahib wrote Tarana-e-Pakistan at the behest of the people with authority in Pakistan." According to Dr. Anjum, Azad Sahib, in an interview, disclosed that he was approached by some high-up officials (possibly from Qaid's office) who wanted him to write Pakistan's national anthem, which they wanted to broadcast on 14th August. However, this was just 5 days before the event, and Azad Sahib initially said it can't be done but then managed to accomplish the task at the 11th hour. The poem was approved by the Qaid within hours and broadcasted the same night.

The call to recognize Azad Sahib's poem as the first anthem of Pakistan has been fervently taken up by human rights activist Beena Sarwar, who also leads the Aman Ki Asha project. In a very well-written article, Beena Sarwar tells us, 'The anthem commissioned by Mr. Jinnah was just one of his legacies that his successors swept aside, along with the principles he stressed in his address to the Constituent Assembly on Aug 11, 1947. A month after his death, the Safety Act Ordinance of 1948, providing for detention without trial – the draft of which Jinnah had in March angrily dismissed as a "black law" – was passed. The following March, the Constituent Assembly passed the 'Objectives Resolution' that laid the basis for recognizing Pakistan as a state based on an ideology.

In all these deviations from Mr. Jinnah's vision, perhaps discarding Azad's poem appears minuscule. But it is important for its symbolism. It must be restored and given a place of honor, at least as a national song our children can learn – after all, Indian children learn Iqbal's 'Saarey jehan se accha'. Such symbolism is necessary if we are to claim the political spaces for resurrecting Mr. Jinnah's vision about a nation where religion, caste or creed "has nothing to do with the business of the State."

While the case of Azad Sahib writing Pakistan's first anthem on behalf of the Qaid looks persuasive, it has been challenged by historian Dr. Safdar Mahmood who writes, "Thinking about the claim by Azad sahib that he wrote the first national anthem of Pakistan, I asked myself, 1. The Qaid had always taken decisions in consultation, so how come, not even knowing much Urdu or Persian, he made a unilateral decision (as claimed by Mr. Azad) to approve this poem as the national anthem of Pakistan? 2. Qaid had lived most of his life in Bombay and Delhi, at the time of the above incident he was around 71 years old, so how come he was aware of a rather unknown Urdu poet of 29 living in Lahore and asked him to write the anthem?"

Dr. Mahmood then goes on to tell us about his research to find evidence supporting Azad Sahib's claim. He refers to a book by Professor Ahmed Saeed titled 'Visitors of Qaid', which covers all those who visited Jinnah till April 1948, and he found that there is no mention of Jagan Nath Azad ever meeting Jinnah. Dr. Mahmood also met Captain Rabani who was the ADC of Qaid during those days and would have known of Jinnah's activities, and Rabani denied Jinnah ever meeting Azad or asking him to write Pakistan's national anthem.

Dr. Mahmood then claims that he thoroughly went through all records and archives of Radio Pakistan and found out that no song or poem written by Azad Sahib was broadcasted by Radio Pakistan between 1st August 1947 and April 1949! According to official records, Dr. Mahmood claims, the first song broadcasted by Radio Lahore after announcing the creation of Pakistan was Ahmad Nadeem

Qasmi's "Pakistan bananay waalay, Pakistan mubarik ho". Neither, he states, is his poem mentioned in any book or journal of that time.

So, what really is the truth? And here I must mention that some other people have also remembered hearing Azad Sahib's poem from Radio Pakistan and thus we are reminded of Oscar Wilde's quote that, "Pure and simple truth is seldom pure and never simple".

This just illustrates how difficult it is to conclusively prove a historical incident just a few years old even when the eyewitnesses are still alive, for memories often get muddled with time and people frequently remember time and dates incorrectly. In the same way records and archives can be doctored and full evidence not disclosed when someone asks for it.

Jagan Nath Azad, who was originally from Mianwali and who very reluctantly left his beloved Lahore in November 1947 to move to India, certainly was in Lahore at the time of partition. And just like I have no reason to doubt the word of the great man Tagore that he did not write Jana Mana Gana to praise the king emperor, I have no reason to disbelieve Azad Sahib that he was asked to write a poem on the occasion of Pakistan's creation. The question is who asked him to do this? And here I very much doubt it was Mr. Jinnah. In fact, I am quite sure that the Qaid was not even aware of any such project. I believe that some of Azad Sahib's friends, who admired his skills as a poet and who may have had links with Radio Pakistan, asked him to write a poem. It is quite possible that this poem, made into a song, was broadcasted by Radio Pakistan (there is no information on who was the singer and who composed the tune), even if it was not the first or even the second song broadcasted on the night of 14th August.

As such, I cannot see Azad Sahib claiming anywhere that he ever met the Qaid personally, and thus Dr. Mahmood's laborious investigation into such a meeting was a bit of a wild goose chase.

Leaving aside the controversy, what I fully accept is that a song in praise of Pakistan was indeed written by Azad Sahib, a Hindu citizen of Pakistan. This poem is part of our cultural heritage, in the same way that Iqbal's "Sare Jahan say Achha" is part of India's cultural heritage, and it is time that we acknowledge this and cherish it. Let us read it and enjoy it:

Aye sar zameen-i-Pak
Zare tere hain aaj sitaron se tabnak
Roshan hai kehkashan se kahin aaj teri khak
Tundi-e-hasdan pe ghalib hai tera swaak
Daman wo sil gaya hai jo tha mudaton se chaak
Aye sar zameen-i-Pak!
Ab apne azm ko hai naya rasta pasand
Apna watan hai aaj zamane main sar buland
Pohncha sake ga is ko na koi bhi ab gazand
Apna alm a hai chand sitaron se bhi buland
Ab ham ko dekhtey hain atarad hon ya samaak
Aye sar zameen-i-Pak!
Utra hai imtehan main watan aaj kamyab
Ab huriat ki zulf nahin mahiv-e-paich-o-taab
Daulat hai apne mulk ki be had-o-be hisaab
Hon ge ham aap mulk ki daulat se faiz yab
Maghrib se hum ko khauf na mashriq se hum ko baak
Aye sar zameen-i-Pak!
Apne watan ka aaj badalne laga nizam
apne watan main aaj nahin hai koi ghulam
apna watan hai rah-e-taraqi pe tez gam
azad, bamurad jawan bakht shad kaam

ab itr bez hain jo hawain thin zehr naak
Aye sar zameen-i-Pak!
Zare tere hain aaj sitaron se tabnak
Roshan hai kehkashan se kahin aaj teri khak
Aye sar zameen-i-Pak!
And to be honest this is as much in Persian as the official anthem!

Breakfast at Faletti's

Faletti's Hotel is one of the iconic landmarks of the great city of Lahore and has an interesting history.

The hotel was opened by an Italian chef, Andrei Faletti. Apparently, his family belonged to the Italian diaspora who left Italy following the Napoleonic wars for various parts of the world. Andrei grew up in London and worked in a hotel there. Inspired by the tales of the Italian adventurer Ventura, who worked as a general for Ranjit Singh and returned to Europe with fabulous wealth, Andrei decided that there was not much future in London and came to Lahore to try his luck, much like people from Lahore now move to London.

It is not known when Andrei arrived in Lahore, but by 1872, he is known to be living in the Bhati Gate area, moving to a flat on Mall Road in 1876. He is also known to have found the bliss of love with a beautiful Lahori courtesan.

After establishing contacts with the British who now ruled Punjab, something in which his Lahori girlfriend played a role, he opened the Hotel fit for a Maharaja, as he so described it, in 1880.

Faletti's Hotel established itself as the best in the city,

and all visitors of substance used to stay there in those days. After the death of Andrei in 1905, the Hotel was taken over by a firm named Associated Hotels of India, which also owned the Cecil's of Murree, Flashman's of Rawalpindi, and Deans of Peshawar.

There was another man who had his eyes on this hotel. His name was Mohan Singh. Born in a village in Chakwal, district Jhelum, now in Pakistan, to poor parents, Mohan Singh studied in Rawalpindi and Lahore but was unable to complete his studies due to lack of financial resources. At one time, he worked in a shoe shop located in Anarkali Bazar, and during this time it is said he came to Faletti's for a cup of tea but due to his shabby attire, the doorman did not let him in, something he never forgot.

Eventually, he became the manager and the owner of a hotel in Simla and founder of a company which established hotels all over India. In 1942 this group bought Associated Hotels of India providing sweet revenge for Mohan Singh whose full name was Mohand Das Oberoi and who had found Oberoi Group in 1934.

It is well known that despite owning many hotels, Faletti's remained Oberoi sahib's favorite, and he frequently used to stay there even after Lahore became part of Pakistan.

In 1965, when war broke out between India and Pakistan, the entire properties of the Associated Hotels Group were taken over as 'enemy property' and handed over to the Pakistan Tourism Development Corporation. Oberoi sahib never got over losing his beloved possession.

The hotel went downhill until it was bought by the present owners in 2000, who restored it, even taking care of the well-known trees in its grounds and recreating the Faletti's of 1880. Over the years, many well-known celebrities including Mohamad Ali Jinnah, Allama Iqbal, Eva Gardner, Marlon Brando, Raj Kapoor, Dilip Kumar, Mohammad Rafi, Garfield Sobers, etc., have stayed here.

The real Bhagat Singh

Jis dhaj say koi maqtal mein gaya woh shan salamat rehti hai
Yeah jan tu aani jaani hai is jan kei koi baat nehein
The pride with which one meets one's end is what lives forever
This life only comes and goes so no need to fuss over it too much.
(Faiz)

On 23rd March 1931, three young men were hanged to their deaths inside Lahore Jail. The British authorities had gone to great pains to do this secretly. The date of execution publicly announced was 24th of March, so many were expecting a last-minute reprieve or stay. After the execution, for which allegedly no magistrate agreed to supervise and an honorary judge was drafted in, the bodies were not handed over to the relatives but removed after making a hole in the back wall of the jail, cremated under cover of darkness at an unknown location, and the ashes thrown in river Sutlej.

These men were Bhagat Singh, aged 23, Sukhdev Thapar, aged 23, and Shivaram Rajguru, aged 22. They had been convicted by a special tribunal in the so-called Lahore conspiracy case that had resulted in the death of an English police officer. The trial and execution produced widespread public interest, and in the case of Bhagat Singh, it brought him everlasting fame which endures even to this day. Countless articles and scores of books have been written on him. He has been the hero of many songs, poems, and plays. Bollywood has been enthralled by him, and many films have been made on him, the most famous being Manoj Kumar's Shaheed in 1965. Leaving aside his movie star fame, Bhagat Singh is widely admired at the grassroots level by the public all over Punjab and beyond.

Of course, this popularity is lot more East of the border where towns and villages have been named after him. West of the border in Pakistan, whose son of soil he was as he was born in Lyallpur district, died in Lahore, and cremated outside Guru Singh Wala village, all areas now in Pakistan, only people who admire Bhagat Singh are a handful of left-leaning Punjabis who have been demanding that the area where Bhagat Singh was executed and is now a major crossing is named Bhagat Singh Square, a demand that Lahore Municipal Authority once accepted before backing out due to a backlash by the Islamist groups.

While at an official level Bhagat Singh does not exist for Pakistan, there is an amusing side to this. When I was in school, I waited for 23rd of March every year with great anticipation and excitement. This is the date on which Pakistan celebrates its National Day to commemorate the passing of the Pakistan Resolution in Lahore by Muslim League in 1940. My reason for looking forward to this day was hardly patriotic. The thing was that on this day a huge military parade was held in Rawalpindi Racecourse Ground. And as in those days I was very keen on military equipment, for me, this was the opportunity to watch all types of tanks, armoured vehicles, guns, etc. rumbling past as one sat in the audience. And by far the most anticipated event was the flypast by Pakistan Airforce led by the in-office Chief in the best fighter aircraft the force had in its inventory.

And so ironically, while at the official level, Bhagat Singh does not exist for Pakistan, in my opinion, without knowing or wanting it, Pakistan continues to pay tribute to him by holding a military parade in his honour, something not even India does!

Some find the popularity of Bhagat Singh surprising. However, for sure it was not just a fluke, and it was something purposely engineered by Singh and his party. The British had in place a very effective system of censorship and therefore Bhagat Singh and his fellow activists were unable to spread their message on a mass scale. To counteract this, Bhagat Singh, who was an educated, intelligent, glamorous, and articulate man as well as good-looking, planned the whole campaign which led to his arrest and trial. Even the famous photograph of him with the stylishly tilted hat was purposely created in Ramnath studio in Delhi a few days before he courted arrest and then distributed widely after the arrest. He knew what it would lead to and was never in doubt that this would be his death, but this was no suicide for the trial gave immense popularity to Singh. It was through this public attention that he was hoping to spread his message on a mass scale.

Unfortunately, it did not achieve the real purpose Bhagat Singh wanted and sadly he was unable to get his message across in its entirety. During the trial, the British tried to portray Singh and his comrades as lunatics. However, the general public concluded that they were anti-colonial freedom fighters, and their death gave them the status of martyrs in the war against British imperialism. While it is a fact that they were genuine anti-colonial activists, that is not the whole story, there was more to Bhagat Singh and his struggle, something that has been lost. Even Bhagat Singh's family (his nephew now heads Bhagat Singh Research Group) have lamented that his real message has been distorted by Bollywood movies.

As a young student in Lahore, Bhagat Singh joined the Hindustan Republican Association (HRA) which had been inspired by the anti-British Republican uprising in Ireland. After this organization suffered significantly due to the crackdown following the Kakori Conspiracy case, Bhagat Singh became one of its leaders. Under his direction, the name of the organization was changed to Hindustan Socialist Republican Association (HSRA), a change that was not just in name but meant significant change in the aim and purpose of the organization.

The point to emphasize is that the portrayal of Bhagat Singh and his comrades as just anti-British, anti-colonial freedom fighters is not correct. What they wanted and for what they gave their lives is best understood by quoting Bhagat Singh's words, "We want a socialist revolution, the indispensable preliminary to which is the political revolution. That is what we want. The political revolution does not mean the transfer of state (or more crudely, the power) from the hands of the British to the Indian." Elaborating on the above point, Singh stated that for workers there is no difference if Lord Reading is the head of the Indian government or Sir Purshotamdas Thakordas, and for peasants no difference if Sir Tej Bahadur Sapru replaces Lord Irwin. He clearly states that what they seek is a real top-to-bottom rearrangement of the Indian society on socialist lines. The slogan which Bhagat Singh and his comrades shouted again and again in court during the trial was 'Inqilab Zindabad (Long live revolution),' not "Azadi, Azadi (Freedom, Freedom)".

So, I am sure Bhagat Singh and his associates would have derived little if any pleasure when the British left in 1947. In fact, quite certainly they would have agreed with those who thought like them, like Sadat Hasan Manto who while the firecrackers are going on outside in Bombay streets at midnight on 15th August 1947 was writing, "Hindustan azaad ho gaya tha. Pakistan aalum-e-wajud mein aate hi azaad ho gaya tha, lekin insaan donon mumlikaton mein ghulam raha, Ta'asub ka ghulam ... mazhabi junoon ka ghulam ... haiwaniyat-o-barbariyat ka ghulam. Hindustan had become free, Pakistan had become free even before it was born. Yet humans in both countries remain enslaved.... slaves of bigotry.....Slaves of religious fanaticism......slaves of inhumanity and barbarity".

And like Faiz Ahmed Faiz who around the same time 900 miles away in Lahore was writing,
"yeh daaġh daaġh ujālā ye shab-gazīda sahar
vo intizār thā jis kā ye vo sahar to nahīñ
najāt-e-dīda-o-dil kī gharī nahīñ aa.ī
chale-chalo ki vo manzil abhī nahīñ aa.ī

This blood-splattered morning, this dark night like dawn
This is not the dawn we were waiting for
The moment of liberation for sight and heart has not yet arrived
March on for our destination has not yet arrived"

Durgha Devi, a freedom fighter from Lahore

Sarfaroshi key tamana ab hamaray dil mein hai
Dekhna hai zoor kitna bazo a qatil mein hai
We are ready to die for our cause now
Let us see how strong is the arm of our killer

(Bismil Azeemabadi)

In the well-known incident on 17th December 1928, revolutionaries Bhagat Singh and Rajguru fired from inside the DAV college, which was across the road, and killed a British police officer who had just left the police headquarters in Lahore. This was to avenge the death of the political leader Lala Lajpat Rai. However, perhaps it is not that well-known what they did next. Both of them escaped from the back entrance of DAV college and went to the house of a fellow revolutionary Bhaghwati Charan Vora, despite knowing he was not in Lahore but had gone to attend the Congress session in Calcutta. At home was his young wife Durga Devi Vora and their son Sachi, who was a few years old. The men, now being hunted by police, asked Durga Devi, who they called Durga Bhabi, for help. Bhagat Charan was a well-off person, and so Durga Devi had a large amount of cash at home which she put at the disposal of the revolutionaries to help them escape, but that was the least of what she did. In fact, she suggested and carried out a daring plan in which she travelled out of Lahore on a train with Bhagat Singh, acting as his wife carrying Sachi in her lap while Rajguru posed as the family servant. And thus, they were able to slip past the police cordon and reached Calcutta safely. When Bhaghwati Charan met them, he was surprised and pleased with the courage and initiative of his wife and remarked, "Now I know that I have a truly revolutionary wife." Considering the social norms of that time when women were not expected to meet men on their own, let alone travel with them, Durga Devi's actions were quite remarkable. Born in a Gujarati Brahmin family, Durga Devi was married to Bhaghwati Charan, who was a couple of years older than her, at the age of 11. Charan inherited a lot of money and after meeting Bhaghat Singh at National College Lahore, he became a revolutionary and a member of Hindustan Socialist Republican Association. Initially, Durga Devi helped the revolutionaries in a supportive role because of her husband, but with time, she herself became a committed revolutionary.

After helping Bhaghat Singh escape, Durga and Sachi returned to Lahore. Soon, police found out about Durga Devi's involvement with the revolutionaries, and she had to go underground to escape arrest. In April 1929, Charan summoned Durga and Sachi to Delhi. There, on 8th April, this family along with Charan's sister Sushila, Azad, and Bhaghat Singh had a picnic in a park where the women fed Singh his favorite foods. Although no words were exchanged about the plan, Durga Devi knew that this would be their last meeting with Bhaghat Singh. From the picnic, Bhaghat Singh went straight to the assembly building where he threw a few firecrackers to draw attention as well as leaflets, raised slogans of Inqilab Zindabad (Long live revolution), and courted arrest. Sushila, Charan, Durga, and Sachi were watching from outside the building and saw Bhaghat Singh brought out in handcuffs and led to the police van. Being a child, Sachi was unable to restrain himself and shouted, "Lamba Chacha (tall uncle)". Startled, Bhaghat Singh looked towards the group, but the police in their haste to get away did not notice and missed the chance to arrest Singh's comrades in arms. When Bhaghat Singh was put on trial, Durga sold her jewellery and led protest processions demanding his release while her husband got involved in a daring plan to free Bhaghat Singh by attacking the police van while he is being transported between jail and court. Unfortunately, on 28th May 1930, while testing a bomb in woodlands near Ravi, Charan died when it prematurely exploded in his hand; he was only 26 years old. Durga Devi was now a widow and on the active list of revolutionaries (to them terrorists) suspects wanted by the police, but she managed to keep one step ahead of them and avoided arrest.

On the night of 8th October 1930, Durga Devi, along with 2 male accomplices, fired from a moving car on an English Police constable and his wife standing outside the police station on Lamington Road, Bombay. Although injured, the couple were fortunate to survive the attack. The eyewitnesses described seeing a long-haired person among the assailants, but the police failed to connect this to Durga Devi as they could not imagine it could be a woman. Durga Devi was finally arrested in September 1932 in Lahore and spent around 14 months in detention. By that time, the Indian Independence movement had become dominated by the Congress, and revolutionaries who used violence to achieve their aims did not have mass popularity.

She, therefore, lost heart in the cause of revolution, and when all charges against her were dropped after amnesty for political prisoners, she returned to teaching. Like other Hindus she had to leave Lahore in 1947. Durga Devi became active in Congress and served in various capacities while continuing to dedicate herself to teaching until well into her 70s. She lived to the ripe old age of 92.

Congress and the Muslim League dominate the narrative of Indian politics leading to 1947, and Gandhi, Nehru, and Jinnah are the names people remember. And while men like Bhaghat Singh are also well-known as peripheral romantic figures in the struggle for independence. Sadly, women like Durga Devi Vora, who took part in the movement side by side with the men, are mostly forgotten.

Source: Revolutionary History of Interwar India by Kama Maclean

Tombs of Jehangir and Noor Jehan

Jehangir was the 4th Mughal emperor who reigned for 22 years (1605-1627). He is buried at Shadara, just outside Lahore. His tomb, a complex of buildings, is considered to be archaeologically the most important Mughal era construction after the Taj Mahal in Agra, and yet no road signs or directions are provided for someone trying to get there! The tomb itself is set within a large garden called Dilkusha Bagh. This was the property of Jehangir's favorite wife and consort, Noor Jehan, and the emperor willed to be buried there. The tomb took 10 years to build and cost 10 lakh rupees, a fortune in those times. There is some dispute among historians, with some crediting his son Shah Jehan and others Noor Jehan with its construction. It is a magnificent building where loads of marble has been used, and the walls are adorned with frescos.

Jehangir fell in love with Noor Jehan, who was from a Persian Shia family, when she was already married (and so was he, but this does not count). Somehow, Sher Afghan, her first husband, died 2 years after Jehangir became the monarch, but it was not until another 3 years that she agreed to marry him. Neither of them were spring chickens, with

Noor Jehan a mature, sophisticated, and strong-willed lady over 30 (Jehangir was 8 years older). It was a perfect marriage, with the assertive queen matched by the weak and indecisive king, who was heavily addicted to opium, wine, and women (though considering the amounts of the first two he consumed, it is doubtful he had much use for the third).

Noor Jehan remains the only Mughal queen who was a joint ruler of the kingdom, for Jehangir consulted her in every important matter, and her approval was required for any decision to become final. She was also the only Mughal female who had coins minted with her name on them. Eventually, she fell out with Jehangir's heir apparent, Prince Khurum, and when Jehangir died and Khuram became Shah Jehan, she retired from public life. She outlived her husband by 18 years.

Shah Jehan's son Aurangzeb had a very close relationship with Noor Jehan. Aurangzeb's real grandmother (Shah Jehan's mother) was a Rajput princess who died when he was only a few months old, and Noor Jehan doted on him. Their affectionate relationship continued until her death when Aurangzeb was 27 years old. It is possible that he learned the art of manipulation and statecraft from her, which enabled him to outmaneuver his other brothers and become the emperor after deposing Shah Jehan. Following this, he made him spend his last years in virtual house (or palace) arrest and in a way paid him back for what had been done to Noor Jehan. Incidentally, Aurangzeb's tomb, built as per his instructions, cost only 14 Rupees and 12 Anans.

Also buried within the garden of Jehangir's tomb is Noor Jehan's brother Asaf Jah, while Noor Jehan and her daughter from her first marriage are buried in a substantial though much smaller tomb a few hundred yards away. A few years ago, Noor Jehan's mausoleum was in bad state, so much so that when poet Tilok Chand Mahroom visited, he wrote a poem that starts with the couplet:

دن کو بھی یہاں شب کی سیاہی کا سماں ہے
کہتے ہیں یہ آرام گہہ نورجہاں ہے

Where even during the day it looks to be night
I am told is the resting place of the Light of the World
Now it has been restored and looks good.

The left-wing poet Sahir Ludhianvi was not impressed with this story of regal love. Just as he wrote a poem on the Taj Mahal presenting it as just a vulgar symbol of a tyrant rather than a temple of love, he wrote one on Noor Jehan's tomb as well, where he portrays her as one of the countless women who had no personal choice but to agree to marry the emperor if he wanted her. Sahir writes what he thinks is the story the mausoleum tells us:

کیسے مغرور شہنشاہوں کی تسکیں کے لیے
سالہا سال حسیناؤں کے بازار لگے
کیسے بہکی ہوئی نظروں کے تعیش کے لیے
سرخ محلوں میں جواں جسموں کے انبار لگے

How to satisfy the lust of arrogant kings
Year after year beauties were sold in the market
How to be the target of lecherous stares
Young bodies were presented in red palaces

So for Sahir Nooe Jehan symbolises the many unknown women used and abused by male kings.

For the love of a Horse

"A horse, a horse! My kingdom for a horse." (Richard III in a play written by Shakespeare)

In 1799, a short, slightly built lad of 19 who had only one eye captured Lahore. Two years later, he declared himself the Maharaja of Punjab. His name was Ranjit Singh.

Arguably, Ranjit Singh created the first and so far only Punjabi kingdom ruled by Punjabis.

A skilled general and administrator, Ranjit expanded his empire in all directions and would no doubt have carved out a much larger part of India for himself if he had not encountered the British in the East and South.

Ranjit used to say that any man who has pride in himself should have the following priorities in his life, and in this order:

1. His horses
2. His work
3. His women

He himself lived by these ethics: he worked hard, enjoyed the company of beautiful women, but above all, loved his horses. His stable had over a thousand horses obtained at great cost. It was said that the monetary value of horses in Ranjit's stables exceeded the value of entire Lahore!

Ranjit was a connoisseur and collector. If he heard about a beautiful horse or a beautiful woman, he would become obsessed with adding them to his collection. For those who become upset by such treatment of women, note we are talking history, not praising Ranjit Singh.

So, in 1822, Ranjit Singh heard that the Burkzai chieftains of Afghanistan possessed a magnificent horse called Asp-i-Lail. The horse was said to be jet black (hence the name, which means a horse as black as the night) with a white patch on its forehead. Besides the fact that this horse was said to be beautiful to look at and fast as lightning, the description matched another famous horse from history: Bucephalus, Alexander of Macedon's favorite steed. And the symbolism of owning a horse like Alexander would not have been lost on Ranjit Singh.

Ranjit Singh's spies told him that the horse was in Peshawar. So, Ranjit, who always preferred diplomacy to war, sent his able foreign minister, Fakir Azizuddin, to Peshawar to negotiate the tribute payment that was to include the horse. Azizuddin informed Chief Yar Mohammed that the Maharaja desired the horse. But when the tribute arrived in Lahore, although there were several horses, Asp-i-Lail was not among them. Angry messages were sent to Yar Mohammed, who replied that he did not have the horse. Further investigations disclosed that Yar Mohammed was indeed hiding the horse. So, after negotiations got nowhere, in 1828, Ranjit Singh sent his army to get what he wanted.

Eventually, after much bloodshed, Ranjit Singh's able French generals Allard and Ventura managed to get the horse for him in 1830. In the process, Peshawar and all of present-day NWFP province west of Attock became part of Ranjit Singh's empire and eventually part of Pakistan at independence.

Now here some may argue that it is rather farfetched to conclude that this war a horse but then was the Trojan war really over Helen?

Ranjit Singh used to say that the horse cost him Rs 6 million (£600,000) and 12,000 men, suggesting that the war with the Afghans was only for the horse, which is unlikely, but the horse may have played a role.

The horse was transported to Lahore in a special carriage. The road it was to travel from Akbari gate to its stables in the Fort had been scrubbed clean for 2 days to make sure there was no dust remaining.

The horse led a luxurious life and was displayed on special occasions when it would wear the Koh-i-Noor diamond around its neck (on the right side as Ranjit could not see with his left eye) while the Maharaja rode on its back.

It is said that after he had a stroke in 1837, paralyzing his right side and affecting his speech, Ranjit Singh, who had long since lost interest in women, only looked happy when he was hoisted onto this horse and took it for a ride.

What happened to it eventually is not clear, and details about it become murky once it came to Lahore. Some sources claim that when they saw the horse, it was not jet black as the name suggests but dark grey with black legs and speculate that the Afghans had deceived Ranjit, giving him the wrong horse. The breed of the horse is also not clear; it was thought to be of Persian or Turkmen stock. Incidentally, Alexander's horse, Bucephalus, is thought to be of Akhal Teke breed, which is Turkmen.

Some sources claim that when the horse died, Ranjit

was alive and buried it with full military honors, including a 21-gun salute. However, no one knows where this horse is buried, unlike Alexander's horse, which became the center of a holy shrine and town. Perhaps because Asp-i-Lail failed to carry Ranjit Singh to world conquest.

A statue of Ranjit Singh riding Asp-i-Lail can be seen at Fortress Stadium Lahore, something that does not make the Islamo-Nationalists happy as they neither like Sikhs nor statues.

Mohammad Rafi

"As a little girl I often rested my head on the lap of my grandmother while she listened to Hindi songs on Radio Ceylon. On one occasion while the song "O dunya kay rakhwalay" was playing I asked her who was the singer and she repled that it was the voice of God, and I looked up at the stars in the sky and said, "God, what a beautiful voice you have!"

(Sujata Dev)

He was born on 24th December 1924 in a village called Kotla Sultan Singh near Amritsar. His father was a respected cook of the village, famous for his Sat Rang Chawal. His full name was Mohammad Rafi, and he was called Pheeko and never had any interest in studies. In 1926, his father moved to Lahore and took up residence in the Bhati Gate area of Lahore, where he opened a dhaba. The rest of the family, including Rafi, moved to Lahore in 1936 and took residence in a 2-room flat in Bilal Ganj. Here, a fakir used to make his rounds regularly, collecting alms and singing, 'Khaidan day din char nein mahi' (Friend, we have just four days to play in life). Young Rafi started to imitate him, and people started commenting that he sings well. He was then sent as an apprentice to his uncle's barber shop as his father was not keen on him becoming a singer. However, as Rafi was not that good at cutting hair, he used to keep customers entertained by singing.

One day in 1943, Jiwan Lall Mattoo, a music executive at All India Radio Lahore, was passing by and heard him humming. He came in and asked Rafi to come to his studio for an audition, which Rafi, to his own astonishment, passed, and from March 1943, became a radio artist. At this stage, Rafi seriously started dreaming of becoming a professional singer, but this may never have happened if it were not for his elder brother Hamid, who decided to support him in every way and arranged for him to learn classical music from recognized ustaads like Ghulam Ali Khan, as well as a range of other singers including folk and qawwali.

Rafi had been married to his cousin Bushra since he was 15, but his father-in-law had told him he would only send his wife to him when he was able to support her, so she had stayed in the village. Now that he had become a radio artist, his wife joined him in Lahore. Although Rafi did sing a couple of songs for movies like Gul Baluch while in Lahore, no one took much notice of him in the film industry. Master Ghulam Haider was one music director who admired his talent, but at the end of 1943, he was moving to Bombay and told Rafi to do the same, and after some reluctance, he decided to do this. Since he had been working and his wife had joined him, Rafi was running an open adda at his home, spending everything he earned on feasting his friends. Now he did not even have money to buy a second-class train ticket to Bombay. His friends pooled in and bought the ticket for him, and he arrived in Bombay in 1945. Unfortunately, his wife refused to leave Lahore, and despite now having a son, their marriage ended.

    Rafi was not an instant hit in Bombay, but certainly his finances improved. While the radio in Lahore paid him Rs 25 for a full day's work, in Bombay he was paid Rs 300 for each song he recorded! He sang in several songs, but mostly as a minor role or as a chorus.

    The first break came when he was asked to record a duet in the film Jugnu with Noor Jehan. The production team for this movie was almost exclusively from Punjab, and so was Noor Jehan, who was already a star. When Rafi arrived to record the song, Noor Jehan laughed and said, 'Tu chhootay, tum Bombay pohanch he gaye, Lahore ka kay haal hai (So little man, you have arrived in Bombay, how is Lahore)?' Rafi, who was known as a quiet man and was visibly nervous, replied, 'Gee Lahore mein sab theek hai aur sab log apne baby Noor Jehan ka intezar ker rahay hain (All is well in Lahore, and everyone is waiting for their baby Noor Jehan)'. Everyone in the studio erupted in laughter at this spontaneous retort. Rafi was not happy with the recording of the song and wanted a retake, but the music director Feroz Nizami said it is fine. When the film was released in 1947, the song was a hit, and Rafi, the star, had arrived. The song was, 'Yahan Badla Wafa kay Baywafai kay Siwa Kya Hai.'

    Thus, started the celebrity career of arguably the greatest singer Indian Subcontinent has produced in modern times, which ended when Rafi Sahib died of a massive heart attack at 10.51 PM on 31st July 1980, aged just 55.

    Rafi Sahib's funeral procession was one of the largest in Bombay's history despite a torrid downpour. Perhaps even God wept at his death. Yet I am sure if there is life after death, Rafi would have been smiling when he watched this

and humming:
>log mere khwabo ko chunkay dalenge afsano mein
>mere dil ki aag bategi dunia ke parwano me
>waqt mere geeto ka khazana dhudhega
>dil ka suna saz tarana dhundhe ga
>mujh ko mery ba'ad zamana dhundhe ga
>People will collect my dreams and put them in stories
>The fire in my heart will be taken up by the moths of the world
>Time will search for the treasure of my songs
>And the silent orchestra of my heart will search for a rhythm

Heera Mandi and Payasa

Heera Mandi (literal translation diamond market) is one of the well-known areas of the old walled city of Lahore. The narrow street with 2 or 3 story houses on both sides was present during the Mughal era, although no buildings from that period survive now. At that time, it was an up-market area inhabited by high-class courtesans who provided entertainment by dance and song. Highly cultured and polished like the Japanese Geishas, providing sexual services was not their norm except to a selected powerful patron. When Ahmad Shah Abdali invaded India in the late Mughal era, his soldiers abducted thousands of women and forced them into sexual slavery. Some of these men set up brothels in the Heera Mandi, and these women would provide sexual service to multiple clients every night while the men pimped for them. These practices continued during the time of Sikhs when fair-skinned Kashmiri girls were easy to buy due to extreme poverty in Kashmir and used until they could be discarded. Despite their claims to be civilized, the British, when they annexed Punjab, did nothing to stop this exploitation of women.

Hameed Akhtar narrates that one day Sahir Ludhianvi

asked him to come with him. They took a tonga and went to Heera Mandi. Along the long narrow street lined with terraced houses on both sides, the courtesans were sitting and inviting customers for a song and dance, maybe more, while outside their pimps jostled with potential clients while guarding them. Hameed Akhtar thought Sahir was in the mood for some entertainment; however, they just walked the entire length of the street at a leisurely pace with Sahir observing what was going on without stopping. After reaching the end, Sahir turned and walked back to the entrance and repeated the whole process again before hopping into a tonga and going home. Hameed Akhtar found this behavior rather peculiar but must have been used to such eccentricities from his friend. A few days later, Sahir read to him his new poem "Chaklay" (Brothels), which he modified years later to create the song for the film Payaasa by S.D. Burman, recorded in the voice of Rafi and filmed on Guru Dutt.

The song talks about the plight of women ensnared in commercial sex trade, often against their will, and what makes it so potent is the repeated question after each atrocity and shame is described, "Jinhein Naz Hai Hind Per Woh Kahan Hain? (Those who take pride in Hindustan, where are they?)" As in, look here, this is the reality of your Hindustan, and what are you doing about it?

So powerful was this message that whoever listened to the song was forced to stop and reflect on it. The song was a big hit all over India; even Prime Minister Pandit Nehru appreciated it, even though it was criticism of his government as well.

Payaasa was released in 1957, which was 10 years after independence. In the days of colonial rule, leaders like Nehru, when coming across the poverty, deprivation, and exploitation of millions, would remark that we are powerless as we are ruled by the colonialists. Once we are free, we will sort out these issues. And here is Sahir, pointing out that after 10 years, nothing has changed. Why is that? In another of his poems titled "26th January," Sahir asks a series of similar questions as to why the situation of the poor has gotten worse since independence instead of getting better.

While some think that the poem "Chaklay" and the film song are the same, there are several changes made to the poem. The main change, of course, is that the repetitive question was changed from "Sana Khwan a Taqdees a mashriq kahan hain (where are those who praise Eastern moral purity)?" to "Jinhein Naz Hai Hind Per Woh Kahan Hain? (Those who take pride in Hindustan, where are they?)"

So, in the 1940s, Sahir was asking the question to the self-styled protectors of Eastern/Indian moral values. Note the line, "Kahan hain kahan hain muhafiz khudi kay?" As we know, Khudi is quite specific to Allama Iqbal, and as Iqbal was sometimes critical of Western values and advised Indians to uphold their superior morality, Sahir in this line is taking a direct swipe at Allama Iqbal listing him as one of the guardians of Eastern values who allow such exploitation of women.

However, by 1957, things had changed. Unlike in the 1940s, the country was now ruled by Indians, and it was now the job of the native rulers to protect their people and the women of their country from exploitation and abuse.

To Sahir's disappointment, nothing had changed. Women were facing the same sexual exploitation and abuse that they did during the time of the Firangi rulers.

In the present time, there are no longer any brothels in

Heera Mandi. One of my friends took me there for a visit (it has some of the best traditional food outlets in Lahore) and announced, "So this is the old Heera Mandi." When I asked, "Where is the new one?" He replied, "In Defence Housing Society."

And while the market where women were bought and sold is no longer at Heera Mandi, as my friend pointed out, the sexual exploitation of women continues in different, more diverse locations.

Koh a Noor (Mountain of Light) in Lahore

There may have been bigger diamonds, but Koh-i-Noor is one of the biggest of all time and certainly the most famous. The diamond has interacted with the city of Lahore several times, and the last such encounter was also the last time it had a home in the Indian subcontinent before it was transported to London, where it remains to this day.

The exact origin of the diamond is unknown, but most likely, it was extracted from the diamond mines of Golconda in the Hyderabad region of India (now Andhra Pradesh) at some unknown time in history. Incidentally, India was the only source in the world of diamonds until the Kimberley diamond mine was opened in 1870.

Although several diamonds mentioned in tales and histories have been suspected of being this one, the first historical record that looks authentic is when it was acquired by Babur's son, Prince Mirza Nasir, during Babur's conquest of North India. Babur allowed the prince, who later succeeded him as Emperor Humayun, to keep the diamond. When Sher Shah Suri forced Humayun to flee westward, he took the diamond with him. Humayun stayed in Lahore for several days before fleeing to Iran, where in order to get support from Iranian Shah Tahmasp, he did two things: converted to Shiaism and gave away the stone as a gift. There were no regulations about toshakhanas in those days, so the Shah kept it as his own without paying any assessed price.

Although Humayun subsequently regained his throne with Iranian help, the diamond remained in Iran until a few years later it mysteriously reappeared in the Hyderabad area. Just how or why is not known. It is speculated that the Safavid Shah of Iran, who was keen to convert as many people as possible to Shiaism, may have gifted it to the Sultan of Golconda as a reward for making Shiaism the state religion of his state.

Somehow, the diamond ended up with the state's Prime Minister, Mir Jumla, and eventually, the Mughal emperor Shah Jahan managed to repossess the diamond by persuading the owner to gift it to him (no toshakhana involved here either). The diamond remained in Delhi until the Iranian warlord turned monarch Nadir Shah arrived in 1739. Nadir remained an unwelcome guest of Mughal Emperor Mohammad Shah, alias Rangeela, for several months. During this time, he collected every valuable item that was in Delhi but could not find the diamond until one of Mohammad Shah's jilted ex-lovers told him that Shah kept it hidden in his turban. Nadir laid out a big party to celebrate his departure from Delhi and, while declaring his brotherly love for Mohammad Shah, announced that they would exchange turbans as per an Iranian ritual of friendship. Later, in his chamber, he unwrapped his new turban and out tumbled the glittering diamond from its folds. "Koh-i-Noor (mountain of light)," exclaimed the bewildered Nadir, and that is the name which has stuck to the stone since then.

As with many of its earlier owners, the diamond was unlucky for Nadir Shah as a few years later he was murdered by his own courtiers. One of his bodyguards, an Afghan who arrived too late to save him, decided to at least rescue the diamond and took it with him to Afghanistan. Later, as Ahmad Shah Durrani, he became the founder of Afghanistan as an autonomous state.

The kingdom established by Ahmad Shah soon fell into disarray after his death due to infighting between his heirs. The diamond changed hands along with the throne of Afghanistan until one of them, Shah Shuja, fleeing from his brother, brought the diamond to India once again. Here, Shuja fell into the hands of Ata Mohammad, the Afghan governor of Kashmir, who put him in prison and tortured him to extract the diamond. This was futile, for earlier Shuja had entrusted the diamond to his principal wife, Wafa Begum, who had travelled to Rawalpindi and sought protection from the Maharaja of Punjab, Ranjit Singh.

Ranjit moved this party consisting of Wafa Begum as well as several other wives and concubines of Shah Shuja to Lahore and housed them in a large haveli. Wafa Begum promised Ranjit Singh that if he rescued and returned her husband unharmed, she would present the diamond to him. For Ranjit Singh, this was a two-for-the-price-of-one deal, as his armies would add Kashmir to his empire under the pretext of rescuing Shuja, and he would become the owner of this fabulous diamond.

However, once he was united with his harem, Shah Shuja forgot about the diamond deal. When reminded, he said he did not have it. Not accepting this nonsense, Ranjit Singh put Shuja under house arrest and stopped any food and sustenance until he coughed up the diamond.

After becoming the proud owner of the Koh-i-Noor,

Ranjit first had it set in his turban and made sure it was done while he watched. He wore this turban 3-4 times before deciding what's the point if he cannot see and enjoy it himself. He then decorated the right side of the bridle of his favourite mount, Asp-i-Lail, with it so that he could see it while he rode. Ranjit, as we know, was blind in his left eye and considered horses his number one favourite possession, even more than women. Finally, as he became older and less able to go for long rides on horses, he mounted it on a bracelet and used to wear it during official ceremonies.

When he was nearing death, Ranjit decided to gift the diamond to a Hindu temple, but his finance minister overruled this and kept it in the royal treasury. Ranjit's empire disintegrated after his death as his heirs fought each other. The British were thus able to defeat the Khalsa army in the Anglo-Sikh wars, and on 29th March 1849, the 12-year-old Maharaja Dalip Singh signed over his kingdom (or more of his father's) and other things to the British in a ceremony held in Shish Mahal of Lahore Fort (the same place where, in the film Mughal-e-Azam, Madhubala aka Anarkali dances singing 'Jab pyar kiya to darna kya').

Surrender of the Koh-i-Noor was one of the specific demands of the British, and according to the agreement signed, Dalip Singh had surrendered it to the Queen of England. The diamond was given to John Lawrence of the three-man Punjab administrative board for safekeeping before it was sent to London for the pleasure of the Queen.

John slipped the box with the diamond into the pocket of his suit jacket, and that evening he changed into a dinner jacket, forgetting all about the diamond. He threw the discarded jacket on a chair and went for dinner.

The next day, during the board meeting with his brother

Henry and Mansel, he was asked if the diamond was safe. Shaken inside, he kept calm and said, "Of course, it was."

As soon as the meeting ended, he rushed home and asked his Indian manservant, who looked after his clothes, if he had found a box in the pocket of his jacket.

The servant said indeed he did. Lawrence asked him to go and bring it quickly and make sure the contents were safe.

When the servant came back, he had the box in his hand and he said, "Here it is, sahib, but there is nothing valuable inside, just a piece of glass."

The diamond was soon transported to London, and there it remains, despite Iranian, Afghan, Pakistani, and Indian governments demanding its return. One wonders what is so attractive about a piece of glass that is thought to bring bad luck!

Hum Jo Tareek Rahon Mein Maray Gaye

In 1960 Faiz wrote a poem called 'Khatm hoi barish-a sang (The rain of stones has ended)'

ناگہاں آج مرے تارِ نظر سے کٹ کر
ٹکڑے ٹکڑے ہوئے آفاق پہ خورشید و قمر
اب کسی سمت اندھیرا نہ اجالا ہوگا
بجھ گئی دل کی طرح راہِ وفا میرے بعد
دوستو قافلۂ درد کا اب کیا ہوگا
اب کوئی اور کرے پرورشِ گلشنِ غم
دوستو ختم ہوئی دیدۂ تر کی شبنم
تھم گیا شورِ جنوں ختم ہوئی بارشِ سنگ
خاک رہ آج لیے ہے لبِ دلدار کا رنگ
کوئے جاناں میں کھلا میرے لہو کا پرچم
دیکھیے دیتے ہیں کس کس کو صدا میرے بعد
'کون ہوتا ہے حریفِ مے مرد افگنِ عشق'
'ہے مکرر لبِ ساقی پہ صلا میرے بعد'

Nagahan aaj meray tar a nazar say kat ker
Tukray tukray hoya afaq pay khursheed o qamar
Abb kissi simt andhayra na ujala ho ga
Bujh gaye dil key tarha rah-a wafa meray badh
Dosto khatam hoi deed-a tar key shabnam
Tham gaya shoor-a junon khatm hoi barish-a sang
Khak-a rah aaj leye hay lab-a dildar ka rung
Koye jana-n mei-n khula meray laho ka purcham
Dekheyae daytay hain kis kis ko sada meray baad
Koon hota hai hareef mei mard afghan a ishq
Hai makarar lab a saqi pay sila meray baad

The poem became very popular, and people asked Faiz, "What is the context of this poem?" Faiz told them that this is a lament for Comrade Hasan Nasir, and most people would say, "Who is that and what has he done to deserve these verses?" Even today, Hasan Nasir remains an unknown and unsung hero.

Syed Hasan Nasir was born in 1928 to an aristocratic family in Hyderabad, Deccan. The great-grandson of Nawab Mohsin ul Mulk, Hasan Nasir became a dedicated follower of communism. When in 1946 the Telangana Rebellion broke out against the feudal landlords, 18-year-old Hasan, instead of living a life of luxury and debauchery on his ancestral wealth, decided to join it, fighting side by side with peasants and Communist Party workers.

In 1950, he migrated to Pakistan while the rest of his family stayed in India and joined the Communist Party, working as a full-time social worker. It always came as a shock to people to realize that he came from an aristocratic and wealthy family of united India. Hasan Nasir had voluntarily chosen a life of poverty, driven purely by a passion for the communist struggle.

When the Communist Party was banned in Pakistan in 1951, he joined the National Awami Party, as this was the only party that opposed the increasing Pakistani movement into the US orbit during the Cold War. Hasan was in and out of prison and was even in exile for one year, but his heart remained with the poor of Karachi, and he kept returning there. In 1957, he became the secretary-general for Karachi.

In 1958, martial law was imposed by General Ayub Khan, who began to suppress all democratic opposition with a special emphasis on communists, whom the newly empowered military and civilian bureaucracy hated with a passion. Seen as agents of the Soviet Union and branded traitors, communists were harassed like no others. Hasan Nasir's fearless criticism of the martial law and Ayub's pro-US policies made him an obvious target. In August 1960, he was arrested and sent to Lahore Fort, which had been converted into an interrogation-cum-torture centre. There he was interned in a cell with no windows and a ceiling height of 5 feet (Hasan was over 6 feet tall). For days on end, he was kept awake by pricking him with needles. During interrogation sessions, his body was burnt with cigarettes, and his nails were removed with pliers. Eventually, after many weeks of brutal torture, he died.

The authorities did not release the news of his death, and this only became public during the proceedings of a habeas corpus petition by Major Ishaq, a week after his death. The prosecution lawyer came up with a story that upon reading his mother's letter which disclosed that his father had become mentally unstable, Hasan Nasir went into shock and later committed suicide. The sentry posted at the cell, the only non-CID employee, was never allowed to testify before the magistrate. The facts of the case were brushed under the carpet, a veil of secrecy descended upon the case and completely stonewalled, Major Ishaq withdrew his petition.

Hasan Nasir's mother, who lived in Hyderabad, learned of her son's murder and came to Lahore. She asked for a post-mortem to be conducted – the military regime tried to block that too, but the courts allowed it. Ayub's government then tried to conceal the location of Nasir's grave. Finally, on orders of the court, it was located, a body was taken out, and his mother was asked to identify her dead son. She refused to acknowledge that the exhumed body was that of her son. The police had disposed of Hasan Nasir's body surreptitiously so that their horrendous torture may never be discovered. His mother returned to Hyderabad Deccan without his body.

So, Hasan Nasir, who was not from Lahore, suffered in Lahore and most likely remains buried in an unknown grave in Lahore.

Smash All the Mirrors

Sadat Hasan Manto, who died on 18th January 1955 in a drab apartment located in Lakshmi Building Lahore, is like a bad penny. No matter how deep you bury him, he keeps coming back. Now and then, someone makes a film on him, and the authorities do not allow it to be screened in Pakistan. Just like his stories, which parents told their children not to read, it is watched by everyone who knows of this ban, even those who had no interest in Manto!

And sometimes an event about him, like Manto Mela, in Alhambra Lahore, has to be cancelled. The executive of Lahore Arts Council who ordered this commented that as long as he is alive, such lewd stuff will not be allowed in Alhambra! I am sure this will also act as something to incite people who never heard the name Manto to start reading his stories!

It is appropriate when talking about Manto to alter a quote by Oscar Wilde, whose play 'Vera of the Nihilists' was one of the first pieces of literature the young Manto translated into Urdu at the start of his career, "There is no such thing as a moral or an immoral short story, short stories are well written or badly written, that is all.' And indeed, as far as the art of writing short stories goes, there is no one who can compete with Manto in Urdu language, something even his enemies agree with.

So what is all this fuss about Manto? Why was he tried six times in his life (3 times before independence from British and 3 after) for writing obscene stories? And if indeed he was such a vile character, why is he so popular? And why do they keep digging up his grave and putting him on trial again and again even though he is dead?

Here we need to understand the various types of people in this world. Essentially, we have those who believe in sweeping everything under the carpet. For them, life is about hiding the bad things. They know this can't be done forever, but they are happy to kick the can down the road for someone else to deal with. As far as they are concerned, it should be "sab acha hai" (all is well).

For the above, Manto and his like are the axe-murderers. These unscrupulous people rub their nose in the crap that is flowing everywhere, and then people demand for this to be fixed. The moralists do not like this, as they have no remedy to fix the moral corruption. Sometimes they are actually party to it; they want everyone to act as if it does not exist. And for them, Manto is something to be avoided like the plague.

We have the realists like Manto. They may not have the solution to the problems of society, but at the same time, they do not believe in hiding the ills of society. For them, the first step in improving ourselves is the realization of what is wrong with us. It is depressing and sad that our society is still controlled by the first type who do not allow us to lay bare the festering sores of our society and thus do not allow any chance for a surgeon to cut away the rotting flesh poisoning the whole body.

Sadat Hasan Manto, an exceptional writer of the realist group, was a man of extraordinary intelligence, with a supernatural ability to understand the psyche of those he met and used to create his characters. But he also possessed the fatal flaw of writing in lucid details the truth about the society he lived in and the people he lived with. As Manto himself confesses, "Dear Lord, please recall from this world Sadat Hasan Manto, for he runs away from fragrance and chases after filth. He hates the bright sun, preferring dark labyrinths. He has nothing but contempt for modesty but is fascinated by the naked and the shameless...." And it was this ability to tell the naked truth without tact that led to the authorities considering him a dangerous progressive and the progressives declaring him to be a reactionary!

In a nutshell, this sums up the relationship Pakistan has with Manto. A man who was born near Ludhiana, that part of India which did not become Pakistan, who found fame, fortune, and friendship in Bombay (not Mumbai as Manto would hate that), another part of India which did not become Pakistan but like many others decided to leave all that to live and love Pakistan but was never accepted or appreciated for this in his life, simply because he spoke the truth without sugar-coating.

Manto does not stop in his evil ways, no sir. When a reader was upset at his write-up about someone dead, claiming that in a civilized society, people do not talk ill of the dead and one should only speak of their virtues, Manto replied, "If that is indeed what happens, then I pronounce a thousand curses on that civilized society and that civilized country where every dead person's character and personality are carted off to a laundry so that they can come back scrubbed clean and white, ready to be hanged under a sign saying, 'Of Blessed Memory.'"

The sad thing is that there is so much in Manto that can help us to come to terms with the events of 1947. For in him, we have someone who hated the very concept of what we call partition but at the same time, someone who accepts it as something that has happened and gets on with life instead of falling into despair due to it.

Yet just like we Pakistanis are in perpetual confusion about what Pakistan is, we are confused about what Manto is, something he saw 67 years ago and is still true, "I feel great sadness today. There was a time when I was considered a progressive, but I was then declared a reactionary. And now, once again, those who had passed the earlier judgment appear willing to admit that I am a progressive. And our government, which pronounced its own judgment over that of others, sees me as a progressive, in other words, a Red, a communist. Sometimes out of exasperation, it calls me a pornographer and files a suit against me. The same government also puts out advertisements in its publications declaring Sadat Hasan Manto to be a great writer of this country, a great short story writer. My melancholy heart trembles that one day this indecisive government will find itself pleased with me and place a medal on my coffin, which would be a great insult to my commitment to what I believe in."

This is exactly what happened in 2012 when the government of Pakistan (then under PPP) woke up from its slumber and bestowed Nishan-e-Imtiaz, the highest possible decoration a civilian can achieve, on Sadat Hasan Manto. An event that must have made him turn in his grave a few times, and having done that, it promptly forgot about him again.

A few years after the above, we had the Supreme Court

banning a film made on his life and some officials banning his planned anniversary celebrations, declaring once again that he is a pornographer!

One is reminded of the verses by Ghalib (Manto's favourite poet written on his tombstone):
"Ya Rub zamana mujh ko mitata hai kiss leyae
Loh-a Jahan pay harf-a-mukarar nehien hon mein
Dear God why does the world want to erase my name
On the face of life I am not a word written twice in error"

The problem is that the more they try to erase it, the more the name Manto keeps coming back to haunt them. And so, what is the solution to this dilemma? How do the pallbearers of morality get rid of Manto once and for all? Well, in my opinion, the only way is to smash all mirrors! For the greatest sin of Manto is that he shows us our real face, with all the warts, blemishes, etc. Only if we smash all mirrors can we be free of all the truth that stares in our face when we look in a mirror. Only then will we be free of Manto and can live in peace.

Bahar Lahori!

A stunning mural adorns a wall inside Punjab University Library and has a verse by the greatest Iranian poet of modern times, Bahar, that roughly translates to:

"Don't even think that anyone on this earth can ever surpass the Iranians for their love for Pakistan." (Translated by Mansoor Irfani)

Mohammad Taqi Bahar (1884-1951) is one of the most influential figures in modern Persian literature. A poet, historian, journalist, and political activist, he is considered one of the five masters who shaped the Persian language as it is today. As a poet, his abilities can be judged from the fact that he was appointed the poet laureate by the then Shah at the age of 19 and given the title of Malek o-Sho'arā (The King of Poets).

In 1905, when the Iranian people began their struggle demanding a democratic constitution from the Qajar rulers, Bahar resigned from his position as the royal poet and joined this movement, during which he was imprisoned by the Shah and likely contracted TB in jail, which later killed him.

For the rest of his life, Bahar worked to enhance Persian

literature through writing and teaching, and he continued to urge Iranians to strive for a democratic country.

During his final illness, one evening a man came to visit him. However, Bahar was sleeping due to his high fever and fatigue. The visitor sat by his bedside for a while and then left.

The next day when he woke up, Bahar felt better. He was told about the visitor from the previous evening, and Bahar composed this couplet:

دوش آمد پئ عیادت من

ملکی در لباس انسانی
گفتمش چیست نام پاک تو

گفت

خواجہ عبدالحمید عرفانی

Dosh amad pay ayadat mann
malaki dar libas insani
Guftmsh cheest naam pak tu guft
Khwaja Abdul Hamid Irfani
Last night came to ask about my health
an angel in the shape of a human
I asked, what is your name, and he said
Khwaja Abdul Hamid Irfani"

The visitor was my grandfather.

Interestingly, Bahar never visited Pakistan. All his knowledge and impressions about Pakistan came from interactions with Pakistanis whom he met in Iran. The closest and most influential of these friends was my grandfather, and Bahar was so impressed by him that he once said that if his house in Iran gets sold, he will buy one in Lahore. Well, that did not happen, but he is here in spirit, as his poetry adorns the walls of the highest institute of learning in Lahore. Thus, Bahar deserves the status of an honorary Lahori, like so many other lovers of this city who had little or no physical contact with it.

A Meeting in Lahore

Early in 1938, Nehru was visiting Lahore when he was invited by Iqbal to his house on Railway Road. Iqbal was not well due to his asthma and other medical problems. The meeting took place on 24th of January 1938. According to those who were present at the meeting, when Nehru arrived, he was received at the door by Mian Shafi and 13-year-old Javed Iqbal. Nehru was led to Iqbal's bedroom, and he walked with his arm around the shoulder of Javed. Iqbal was lying on the bed, and as a mark of respect, Nehru refused the chair that was offered and sat on the carpeted floor.

They talked about a range of subjects. Most of the talking was done by Iqbal, and Nehru listened respectfully.

It is interesting that Iqbal asked Nehru how many of his fellow congressmen agree with his socialist ideas? Nehru replied about half a dozen, and Iqbal remarked, "How do you expect 10 crore Muslims to be convinced by your advice to trust Congress when you cannot even convince more than 6 of your own party?" Nehru had no answer to this, and neither have those who want to put the entire blame for partition on Jinnah and Muslim League.

Iqbal's affection for Jawaharlal Nehru is well known. The Brahmin Kashmiri connection was a natural bond; in addition, both shared the distinction of being failures at practicing law but becoming towering figures in literature and politics, respectively.

Iqbal once wrote these verses:
'Hind ra in'n zauk Azadi ki dad'h?
Said'h ra sau'dai sayadi ki dad'h?
Un'n Brahmin zadan zindah dil
Lalia'h ahmar rau-shou'n khajil
Who gave Hind/ India zest for freedom?
and who turned the hunted into hunters?
They were the lively sons of Brahmins
whose radiant faces put the sparkling stones to shame!
Tez been puktah kar va sakht koosh
Az nigah'shoun far'hangh un'derh kharush
Asil shou'n az khakh damangir ma aast
Mat'lah akh'taran Kashmir maa aast!
Vigilant dexterous and ever striving
  their sharp vision made Western imperialists look inwards
Their essence comes from my enchanting land
for the galaxy is full of stars from our Kashmir'

Iqbal wrote the above verses to highlight the role Kashmiris played in India's struggle for freedom. In particular he praises radiant faced sons of Brahmins. It is speculated that he was specifically aiming at Motilal and Jawaharlal Nehru, but it is also likely that he included himself and others like Tej Bhadur Sapru, Kailash Nath Khatju, Rattan Nath Sarshar etc. as among these stars.

Years later, in his book, The Discovery of India, Nehru has recalled his meeting Iqbal with affection. There are two remarks in the book on Iqbal that need to be looked at.

Nehru claims that Iqbal said to him, " The difference between you and Jinnah is that he is a politician and you are a patriot."

While only Iqbal knows what exactly he meant these words can and have been interpreted in many ways. Nehru certainly took it as praise for himself and a snub for Jinnah, yet was it so? One of my learned friends Professor Ishtiaq thinks so and says that the word politician is a derogatory term and used in a negative sense, if praise is intended then he would have used statesman. I disagree, according to the World Book Dictionary, "Politician is a person who gives much time to political affairs; a person who is experienced in politics and a statesman is a person who is skilled in the management of public or national affairs."

And although many have expanded on this subtle difference to illustrate the much greater practical difference the impression, I get is that a statesman is like a more senior, advanced and higher grade of a politician, a bit like a physician becoming a professor. To achieve the status of a statesman a politician must prove by his ideas, vision, and performance that he can be called a statesman. Now in January 1938 neither Nehru nor Jinnah could be called statesmen as neither had made any significant impact on the world. They were both spending considerable time of their lives on politics and hence both should be called politicians. However, the fact that Iqbal only called Jinnah a politician was in my opinion a slight snub on Nehru whose life was obsessed with politics.

Furthermore, calling Nehru a patriot does not automatically mean that he was calling Jinnah unpatriotic. As far as I can see, Iqbal did not use the term politician in a negative way but simply told Nehru that Jinnah has an edge over him in this field while he has no doubt about his

(Nehru's) patriotism.

Nehru then (in his book) quotes Edward Thompson who has attributed these words to Iqbal, "Pakistan will spell disaster for Hindus, Muslims, and the British Government. But I am the president of the Muslim League, and therefore it is my duty to support." And with this, Nehru has tried to portray that Iqbal had completely washed his hands off his role in the idea of an autonomous Muslim state in India and that he was not agreeing with the politics of Jinnah and the Muslim League.

While people say different things at different times, it is hard to agree with the narrative of Thompson. Two letters from Iqbal to Jinnah, dated 28th May 1937 and 21st June 1937, are available in which he ridiculed the newly framed constitution of the United Federation in India, asking Jinnah to put in a plea for self-governing Muslim States in North-West and North-East. Also, during Iqbal's lifetime, Jinnah and the Muslim League had never made the demand for Pakistan.

The meeting between Nehru and Iqbal did come to a rather abrupt end when Mian Iftikhar-ud-Din suggested that things might turn out better if Iqbal were to take over the leadership from Jinnah. Iqbal became rather upset at this, got up from his bed, and admonished Mian Sahib, telling him that only under Jinnah have the Muslims achieved some sort of unity and he regards Jinnah his leader and himself just one of his soldiers. Sensing the tension at this stage, Nehru excused himself and left.

There is no doubt that some disagreements did exist between Iqbal and Jinnah. The foremost was Iqbal's repeated plea to Jinnah to start a program of social and economic uplift for Muslims side by side with his political struggle for their rights. Iqbal was afraid that in post-British

India, the Muslims would be rendered voiceless and sidelined due to them being a minority that was backward and poor and would be exploited by Hindu and Muslim feudal.

Iqbal was apprehensive that unless a plan for social change is outlined by Jinnah along with the demand for an independent state such a state if achieved will be only the transfer of power from gora sahib to brown sahib but the majority of Muslims remaining power and oppressed. As we can see these fears have been realised.

Ghazi Ilam Din and Jinnah at Lahore High Court

Ghazi Ilam Din is considered the prototype of those who are actually Shaheed but are called Ghazi (these are contradictory terms as Shaheed dies is battle and Ghazi comes out of it alive). A lot of myths have been created about Ilam Din to make him look like a lion-hearted man of valor defending the honor of Prophet Mohammad.

The truth is far less glorious.

As the story goes, a Hindu named Rajpal from Lahore had published a pamphlet titled, "Rangila Rasul" which allegedly insulted Prophet Mohammad. A case was registered against him for blasphemy but after a 5-year trial, he was acquitted in 1929. The Muslim community was very resentful of this, even though the author of the piece whose identity had been kept secret had allegedly done it in retaliation to another publication by a Muslim in which goddess Sita had been portrayed as a prostitute. And though Rajpal had not written the pamphlet himself, being the publisher, he was the obvious focus of the Muslim anger. Ilm Din, born in 1908, was a poor, illiterate son of a carpenter also living in Lahore. His friend Sheeda had a shop in front of Wazir Ali Mosque and one day when passing near the Mosque they heard several people who had just come out from Jumma prayer talking about killing someone. On inquiry, they were told that a Hindu Rajpal had insulted the prophet and the Mulana in the sermon had asked the faithful to kill him. Ilm Din and Sheeda decided that they should undertake this glorious expedition. Ilm Din purchased a dagger for one rupee and went to Rajpal's shop on 6th September 1929 and stabbed him to death. According to the story, he stood by the corpse and proudly declared that today I have avenged my prophet in front of the whole bazar and then presented himself to police for arrest.

Subsequently, the prominent Muslim lawyer M.A. Jinnah volunteered to defend him in court. Jinnah asked Ilam Din to enter a not-guilty plea, but Ilam Din refused and confessed he had killed an enemy of Islam and was ready for the gallows for this. So he was convicted and hanged. Apparently, his funeral was one of the largest in Lahore's history, and many prominent Muslims, including Allama Iqbal, attended and said nice words about him. He was named Ghazi Ilam Din Shaheed, which is a contradiction for one can either be a Ghazi or a Shaheed, but nevertheless, he is both! It is also stated that this was the only case Jinnah lost in his career.

Well, as the case proceedings were recorded and available in archives, a rather different story emerges from a read. In actual fact, Jinnah was not the defense lawyer at all. As Ilam Din was penniless, the court had appointed a Lahori, Farukh Hussain, to defend him. As the case started, Farukh Hussain entered a not-guilty plea for his client. Therefore, the tale of Ilam Din bravely owning up to his act is a fallacy. The defense did not produce any witnesses during the trial; the prosecution produced two. Kidar Nath and Bhagat Ram, both worked at Rajpal's shop, and according to their evidence, they saw the accused running away with Rajpal on the floor, so they chased him. He was finally caught when he went into a blind alley. He then declared that "Today I have avenged my Prophet" before he was overpowered. The court accepted the testimony of these witnesses and condemned Ilam Din to death. There is no evidence of Ilam Din making any verbal statement in the court; however, his lawyer entered an appeal on his behalf for which Ilam Din would have given permission.

Only then did Farukh Hussain approach Jinnah, who agreed to represent Ilam Din at the appeal trial, and for this, he stayed three weeks at Flatties Hotel room number 18. It is worth noting that Jinnah could not have asked Ilam Din to plead not guilty since he had already pleaded not guilty. Jinnah's argument was based on technical issues which were, "that Kidar Nath was not a reliable witness because (1) he was an employee of the deceased and, therefore, interested. (2) He had not stated in the First Information Report (a) that Bhagat Ram (the other witness) was with him, and (b) that the appellant had stated that he had avenged the Prophet. As to Bhagat Ram, it was contended he, as an employee, was interested, and as to the rest that there were variations in some of the details." The court rejected these arguments. Jinnah then pleaded "that the sentence of death was not called for and urged as extenuating circumstances, that the appellant is only 19 or 20 years of age and that his act was prompted by feelings of veneration for the founder of his religion and anger at one who had scurrilously attacked him." This was rejected as well due to precedence that age, etc., are not to be considered as an argument for such cases. The appeal court maintained the sentence, and Ilam Din was hanged in

Mianwali Jail on 31st October 1929. Once again, there is no evidence of any statement, verbal or written, by him during or after the trial. No last words by him have been recorded in the jail documents.

Lala Amarnath, the swashbuckler from Lahore

Although the British refused to give India the status of a self-governing dominion, somehow they did give her the status of a test-playing nation. India played her first test at Lord's in 1932. Following this, in 1933-34, the English team was to tour India, and the first home test was scheduled to take place in Bombay starting on 15th December 1933. For selecting the team, trial matches were held, and one of the hopefuls was a 22-year-old young man from Lahore called Lala Amarnath Bharadwaj. He was sent to open in both innings of the match and failed miserably. And while he was packing his stuff to go back to Lahore, a fellow Lahori, the giant fast bowler Mohammad Nisar, came to his aid. Nisar, who was already a star player for India, felt that Amarnath had not been given a fair trial as his normal batting position was one down. So he begged, cajoled, and threatened the selectors, convincing them to give Lala Amarnath one more chance. And so they called him for the second trial game where he batted at number 3 and scored 49 and 79 not out to get selected for the test match. The rest, as they say, is history. In the test match, Lala batting at number 3 top-scored with 38 in India's first inning score of 219. Then in

India's second inning, he came in with the score 9 for 1 and 210 more needed to avoid an innings defeat. Lala took on the English bowling like a wolf in a chicken coop, cutting, hooking, and driving. He scored his first 83 runs in 78 minutes before slowing down as he approached the landmark to become the first Indian to score a test hundred, reaching the milestone in 117 minutes. Eventually, he was out for 118 scored with 21 fours. Although India lost the match, Lala Amarnath became a romantic hero for entire India. Women offered him their jewellery, and Rajas offered parcels of money. Years later, in 1955, Amarnath, by then retired after captaining India and now the manager of the Indian touring side to Pakistan, recalled this incident during a press conference in Lahore. He confessed that had it not been for Nisar, he may never have had a chance to play for India. However, this connection with a fellow Lahori is not the only debt Lala Amarnath had to Lahore; it is much deeper than that.

Cricket came to Lahore, like the rest of India, along with the conquest of the colonial power. The British soldiers played cricket in the city as early as 1846, but it was the establishment of the Gymkhana Cricket Club in 1880, with its still picturesque ground just off Mall Road, that formally established the game in the city. Initially, it was an exclusive club for high-ranking civil and military officers, and lower-ranking officials established their own Anarkali Cricket Club.

The game soon spread beyond the officials of the Raj to the common people of Lahore and among the various educational institutions of the city. Atchison College, Government College, and Islamia College all had cricket teams they were proud of, and two cricketing clubs dominated the club scene: the Mamdot Club, which had princes and feudal members, and the Crescent Club, which contained people from the evolving business and middle class of Lahore. The fierce rivalry between these two provided a healthier outlet for the class tensions simmering in the city.

The Crescent Club played at Minto Park (now called Iqbal Park, where the Minar-e-Pakistan stands), and its main sponsors were the Rana family from the Mochi Gate area. One day, the patriarch of the family, Rana Tawakkal Majid, was walking back from a match when he saw a few boys playing street cricket. A lad who was batting executed a perfect cover drive. Rana Sahib stopped and asked him to do this again, which he did at the next ball. Impressed, Rana Sahib inquired about the boy and found that he was from a Brahmin family of modest means who lived in the Shah Alami area of Lahore. Rana Sahib offered that the boy to move into their family home, and so Lala Amarnath came to stay with a Muslim family for the next few years of his life. During this time, he developed into a star cricketer for Crescent Club, winning many trophies for them. He never forgot the kindness of strangers, and whenever after partition he visited Lahore, he came to pay his respect to the house he lived in. Once, he came with his two sons and bowed with reverence at the threshold, asking them to do the same.

Lala Amarnath's story is another example of the tolerance Lahoris had in those days. Unlike Bombay, where cricket teams were formed along communal-religious lines, in Lahore, they were mixed teams with people of different religions playing on the same side.

Lala Amarnath went on to captain India and played a leading role in Indian cricket even after he retired. In 1952, when Pakistan and India played their first Test Match in Delhi, they were captained by AH Kardar and Lala

Amarnath, both from Lahore, who used to live near each other in the Bhati Gate area.

And while Lahore may have helped him become a star, it was his Lahoriat, which includes a disdain for authority when it is being unfair, that caused him problems in life. In the 1936 tour to England, Lala looked with disgust at the way the Indian princes and rajas controlled the team, and one day when he was ready to bat, all padded up and was told that other players would be sent ahead of him, he lost his cool and gave a mouthful to the captain, a rant no doubt laced with the choicest four-letter words Lahoris are so fond of. He was sent back to India for indiscipline, which damaged his career as there were already so few opportunities to play tests in those days. Lala only played 6 tests before World War 2 started, and when test cricket resumed for India after that, he was 35 and past his peak as a player. Still, he became the first and only bowler who got the greatest, Don Bradman, out hit wicket!

As one of his colleagues said about him, 'Lala was quick to love and quick to fight,' a trait which is prevalent among those from Lahore. Alas, that tolerance no longer forms a trait of Lahoris. The end of it can be marked by the day when a mob burnt the home of Amarnath family during the partition madness, though fortunately, Lala was in Poona for cricket trials.

یہ جشن جشن مسرت نہیں تماشا ہے
نئے لباس میں نکلا ہے رہزنی کا جلوس
ہزار شمع اخوت بجھا کے چمکے ہیں
یہ تیرگی کے ابھارے ہوئے حسیں فانوس

ye jashn jashn-e-masarrat nahīñ tamāshā hai

na.e libās meñ niklā hai rahzanī kā julūs
hazār sham-e-uk̲huvvat bujhā ke chamke haiñ
ye tīrgī ke ubhāre hue hasīñ fānūs
This is not a celebration of joy but a farce,
The gang of robbers has just changed uniforms,
After extinguishing a thousand candles of tolerance have become bright,
These embossed beautiful chandeliers of darkness.

(Sahir Ludihanvi on the Independence celebrations, 14-15 August 1947)

From Russia with love to Lahore

Sir Ganga Ram is well-known in Pakistan and admired for designing and building many of the landmarks of modern Lahore. He was a native son of Punjab from the Sheikhupura District. Another man who played a prominent role in building Lahore but does not get the recognition he deserves was from Russia, his name was Nasreddin Murat-Khan, and he was born in 1904 in the Dagestan region of the Russian Caucasus.

Murat-Khan studied Civil Engineering and architecture and worked for the Russian government but his desire to free the Caucasus from Stalinist Russia endangered his life and he escaped to Germany in 1944. He stayed there for 6 years in a refugee camp run by UNO for displaced people. Here he met Hamida Akmut who had a Pakistani father and Austrian mother. Hamida was studying medicine in Vienna when due to war she was evacuated to the refugee camp in Germany, they got married and in 1950 moved to Lahore where Hamida's parents had settled, her father Dr. Abdul Hafiz being from an established and prosperous family of Lahore.

For the next 20 years till his death in 1970, Murat-Khan

worked as an architect, initially for the government of Pakistan designing many buildings including Nishtar Medical College Multan, Textile College Faisalabad, and Lahore Stadium (now called Ghaddafi Stadium) and Fortress Stadium.

Later, he formed his own firm of architecture and town planning. It was then that Murat-Khan built his most well-known project, the Minar-e-Pakistan, which stands in the park where the Pakistan resolution was passed in 1940. The fee due to Murat-Khan for the project was Rs 2,53,883, which he did not claim, donating it to the fund created for financing the project by the Governor of West Pakistan. By this generous gesture, Murat-Khan thanked the city of Lahore, which gave him a new home, accepting him as one of her own.

There is an interesting side story to this tale. Soon after Pakistan was created, my grandfather Abdul Hameed Irfani was appointed the first Press and Cultural Attaché in Tehran, Iran. Without much help from the consulate, he started the task to promote and cultivate Pakistan among the Iranians by highlighting the long-standing and strong cultural ties between the two peoples. He developed friendships with many Iranians, among them was a paediatrician, Dr. Ketchkinay Kazmi, who became a close family friend. Dr. Kazmi had a Russian mother and an Iranian father; she was highly cultured and spoke seven languages.

Dr. Irfani wanted to establish an Iran-Pakistan Cultural Institute in Tehran. After the Pakistani embassy declined to provide any financial assistance, Dr. Kazmi generously offered to host the literary meeting of the Institute at her own spacious family home, bearing the expenses from her own pocket. An extremely kind and generous person, Dr.

Kazmi used to collect leftover food from any party she attended and then personally went out to feed the stray cats and dogs in the streets of Tehran.

A few years later, as the president of the Iran-Pakistan Cultural Institute, she was invited to visit Pakistan, where she visited various cities and met many prominent Pakistanis, including Faiz Ahmed Faiz. Dr. Kazmi fell in love with Lahore and, with the help of contacts in Lahore, purchased a plot of land on what is now MM Alam Road to build a house there. During another visit to Pakistan with an RCD team, she attended a function where Murat-Khan was also present. Most likely, they were the only people there who could speak Russian, so they started a conversation and discovered that Dr. Kazmi had a friend in Tehran who was Murat-Khan's sister and had moved to Iran due to the war. Murat-Khan then designed and built a beautiful house for Dr. Kazmi in Lahore. As things turned out, Dr. Kazmi, who visited Lahore a few more times, never actually lived in the house, which was initially rented to the in-laws of one of Murat-Khan's daughters. Eventually, Dr. Kazmi sold the house to them, and subsequently, it was bought by Hanif Jewellery and Watches, who opened their showroom at that site in 1978.

Amrita and Lahore

'There were two kingdoms only:
the first of them threw out both him and me. The second we abandoned.
Under a bare sky
I for a long time soaked in the rain of my body, he for a long time rotted in the rain of his.
Then like a poison he drank the fondness of the years. He held my hand with a trembling hand.
"Come, let's have a roof over our heads awhile.
Look, further on ahead, there,
between truth and falsehood, a little empty space.'

Amrita Kaur was born in Gujranwala. She lost her mother when she was 11 years old and was brought up by her father under the supervision of her deeply religious grandmother. Perhaps because they lived in Lahore, the most tolerant city of India at that time, Amrita's free spirit was nurtured. Even as a child, she questioned the religious bigotry she saw, as she narrates:

"In the kitchen, grandma ruled, and my first rebellion was against this government. I used to see that in a corner of one shelf are kept three glasses separate from all others.

These glasses were only used when my father's Muslim friends visited, and they were offered tea or lassi. After that, they were washed and put back in their corner. So I joined these three and became the fourth glass, and us four took on grandma. These glasses could not touch any other utensil, so I declared that I will also not touch any other utensil and only drink in one of them. Grandma could keep the glasses separate but could not let me die of thirst, so the crisis was escalated to my father. He was not even aware that these glasses are kept separate, and when he found out, my rebellion became successful. And then no utensil remained Hindu or Muslim.''

After marriage to Pritam Singh, who owned a shop in Anarkali, Amrita Pritam became a famous poet admired not just for her poetry but also for her beauty. As a Bombay scriptwriter who met her observed, 'Amrita Pritam was a chiselled piece of marble. If a sculptor's eyes had fallen on her, he would have carved a statue out of her that would have been worshipped as Radha in temples today.'

Her rebellion against the division of humans along religious lines continued as she once wrote, 'I realized and gathered the moot difference between a Brahmin and myself, precisely that I am not a Brahmin. That's also the difference between a Kshatriya and myself that I am not a Kshatriya. Similarly, that's the difference between a Vaish and myself that I am not a Vaish. And then it also dawned that there's a similar difference between me and a Hindu, Sikh, or Muslim—that I am not a Hindu, Sikh, or Muslim.'

Among her closest friends was the poet Sahir Ludhianvi, whom she first met at a poetry meeting in Preet Nagar, a place halfway between Lahore and Ludhiana where Sahir was a student. From Amrita's writings, it looks as if she was strongly attracted to Sahir from that first meeting. Not long after that, Sahir was forced to leave his college, and he moved to Lahore. Amrita lived in a house on Dhani Ram Road, and if we follow this road East, it curves South in front of King Edward Medical College to become Ewing Road, which goes past Neela Gumbad (Blue Dome) fountain to join Mall Road, the Champs-Élysées of Lahore in those days.

Sahir was known to visit this house frequently. Just what was the exact nature of the relationship between him and Amrita is unknown, for Amrita was married and lived in the house of her husband and extended family. However, it is certain that Amrita acted as the muse for Sahir to write many of his poems, which he published as the collection 'Talkhian,' while both thrived in the vibrant, multicultural, multi-ethnic, literary, and romantic Lahore of those days.

Unfortunately, dark clouds were gathering over the horizon, and soon the madness of religious fanaticism engulfed India, spreading to Lahore and shattering the lives of those living there, including Amrita, who tried to warn people of the dangers with her poetry.

'When religion goes to people's heads-
Steel is sharpened,
People's tongues grow cruel,
The tongues of love grow dull,
Veins flowing with red blood turn blue,
From their hiding places behind every bush,
Poisonous snakes come slithering out to bite,
And lips once beautiful to kiss begin to foam.
Vultures gather, their beaks tearing at the bodies,
They don't care if it's the daughter or the,
daughter-in-law of the house.
In bright daylight and pitch darkness of night
Steel is sharpened,
Innocent children,

Delicate women and strong young men,
Are sacrificed at the altar of this passion.
When the frenzy of religion goes to people's heads'

Her words fell on deaf ears as Punjab, including Lahore, dissolved into a frenzy of burning, looting, rape, and murder. Afraid for her safety and for her family, and not knowing if there would be a midwife available when she went into labour as she was expecting, Amrita left Lahore with a heavy heart. She thought it would only be for a few days. Her biggest concern was being separated from her friends, as she writes,

"I left Lahore after the dreadful riots of March-April 1947. It never crossed my mind, even for a minute, that I would not be able to return, and I left all my jewellery with our trusted servants. My biggest concern when leaving was to lose two of my most cherished friends, Sajjad Zaheer and Sahir Ludhianvi. I did not take any winter clothes, as we thought it would all be settled by then.

Alas, this was not so. By winter, it was clear that there would be no going back to my beloved Lahore."

On the way to Amritsar and then Delhi, what she saw and experienced made her realize that the world had changed forever, and she would never again come back to Lahore. It was a devastating experience, and she found it hard to explain how this metamorphosis took place. The best explanation she could think of was in the words of her most famous poem,

'Rise! O' narrator of the grieving;
rise! look at your Punjab,
Today, fields are lined with corpses,
and blood fills the Chenab,
Someone has mixed poison,

in the five rivers' flow,
Their deadly water is, now,
irrigating our lands galore,
This fertile land is sprouting,
venom from every pore,
The sky is turning red,
from endless cries of gore'

Amrita never visited Lahore again. She knew that the Lahore she loved did not exist anymore. It was now an alien place that was intolerant and bigoted towards those who were of the wrong religion. Like many others who were displaced from their homes during that time of madness, Amrita severed her ties from any specific place that she would call home, as she tells us,

'Today I have erased the number of my house
and removed the name of identity from my street's forehead
and have wiped off the directions on each road
But if you really want to find me
then knock at the door of every country
every city, every street
and wherever you see the glimpse of a free spirit
..........That will be my home'

When Tagore called

In 1934, Rabindranath Tagore, the first non-Western writer to win the Nobel Prize for literature, visited Lahore. I do not know why he did so. Maybe he had heard the saying that the person who has not seen Lahore has not lived and wanted to do this before it was too late. After all, he would have turned 73 that year. How long he stayed is also not known.

However, we know that he stayed with his friend Dhani Ram Bhalla in his mansion at Nawa Kot, Lahore. Bhalla Sahib, who is a legend in himself, was a high-caste Hindu from Hoshiarpur who broke social taboos by starting a leather business. It looks as though Bhalla Sahib is another example of high-caste Hindus who were ostracized for breaking taboos and found acceptance and tolerance in Lahore. "Bhallay Di Hatti," the name of his shoe shop in Anarkali Bazaar of Lahore, became one of the most popular shoe shops in India. Saadat Hasan Manto mentions that when he and Ismat Chughtai had to visit Lahore a few times to attend their trials for vulgar writing, buying shoes at Bhallay Di Hatti was something they looked forward to and spent hours there.

Dhani Ram Road still exists in the Anarkali area of Lahore though Bhallay Di Hatti was burnt during the madness of 1947.

What Tagore's activities in Lahore were not clear, but we do know that one day he went to see Iqbal at his residence at 116 McLeod Road. Unfortunately, Iqbal at that time had gone to Bahawalpur, so no meeting took place.

When Iqbal came back, he was informed of Tagore's visit and his desire to meet him. However, he never tried to contact Tagore, never wrote to him, or anything. How strange! Why?! No one knows for sure, though many have often wondered why. Regardless of the reason, a great chance for possible collaboration between two great minds was missed.

Without a doubt, Tagore and Iqbal are the two greatest 20th-century poet-philosophers from the Indian Subcontinent.

There is a lot of overlap between their philosophy and poetry, though Iqbal at times writes in terms of Islamic-specific poetry while Tagore remained, by and large, a pantheistic/mystic poet throughout his life.

On his part, Tagore mentioned Iqbal on several occasions and always spoke highly of him. Once, while talking to one of Iqbal's friends, he asked if Iqbal wrote in Punjabi. When he was told no, and that Punjabi was not a language but a dialect, Tagore remarked that this was most unfortunate. He believed that if someone of Iqbal's calibre had written in his native language, it would have established Punjabi as a major literary language. This may well be true, as we can see that men like Pushkin and Tagore were responsible for the literary birth of Russian and Bengali languages.

Perhaps what Tagore did not realize was that Iqbal was

not a typical poet. Unlike most poets who use their mastery of words and languages to produce poetry even on demand, beautifying it through correction and revisions, Iqbal was unable to write a single line of poetry at will. Instead, once in a while, more or less spontaneously, he would produce a torrent of outstanding poetry, in Urdu in his early years and Persian later. He would recite this poetry from memory, never writing it down on paper.

In a letter to Iqbal's friend Dr. Abbas Ali Khan dated February 7, 1933, Tagore writes:

"Your letter and poem have touched my heart. It has given me deep pleasure to know that you have found an inner affinity between my poems and those of your great poet Sir Mohammad Iqbal. Not knowing the languages in which he writes his original poems, I am not in a position to reach the depths of his creative production or to properly evaluate them. But I am assured through the wide fame they have won that they carry the majesty of eternal literature. It has pained me often to find a certain class of critics trying to create misunderstanding by ranging my literary works against those of Sir Mohammad Iqbal on a competitive basis. This is an entirely erroneous attitude to take towards literature that deals with the universal. I am sure both myself and Sir Mohammad Iqbal are comrades working for the cause of truth and beauty in literature and meet in a realm where the human mind offers its best gifts to the shrine of Eternal Man."

Among their respective followers, there have been attempts to compare them with each other, even in competitive terms. Such attempts are always difficult as they wrote in different languages and generally had somewhat different attitudes toward the events of their times. As we can read above, Tagore himself was unhappy with such attempts.

Some also think that Iqbal had resentment about Tagore receiving the Nobel Prize, but it seems that it was Iqbal's admirers who were more unhappy about this than Iqbal. It should be noted that when Iqbal's collection of books was catalogued, six English translations of Tagore's works were part of the collection. So, what can we make out of the conflicting attitudes of these giants toward life and towards each other? Well, I think we need to analyse and evaluate them considering what these two were in personal terms.

Tagore was born in a well-off household, his family had land and money. He did not need to struggle to make ends meet. Tagore did not even complete his formal education, knowing he was not dependent on a job for income, and devoted his life to literary pursuits from his youth.

Iqbal had no such luck; he had no family fortune and struggled all his life to provide for himself and his family. Iqbal had to complete formal education and acquire the skills of a solicitor to find work.

Tagore was born into a reformist Hindu household, while Iqbal was born into a conservative Sunni Muslim household.

The above factors seem to have influenced the works and attitudes of Tagore and Iqbal. Not having to face the harsh realities of life as far as putting food on the table is concerned, Tagore retains his gentle, generous, and magnanimous soul. Iqbal, on the other hand, frustrated with the need to balance time for income-generating work with his literary passion, perhaps developed a hardness and even some bitterness which spills over in his work and attitude towards Tagore. Added to this was that Iqbal was part of the minority Muslim community of India and had the defensive attitude minorities tend to develop, especially if they believe they are being threatened.

As Rafiq Zakria sums up, "Tagore brought out the romantic in man; Iqbal the heroic. Tagore exulted in feminine beauty; Iqbal in masculine strength. There was music in Tagore's poetry; there was fire in Iqbal's. Tagore was humble; Iqbal was proud. Tagore was always active; Iqbal easy-going and lazy."

The last lines come directly from a rare mention of Tagore by Iqbal, who more or less ignores the existence of Tagore, at least publicly, but once remarked to CV Raman, the renowned physicist and Nobel Laureate, that "Tagore preaches rest but practices action; Iqbal practices rest, preaches action."

This is an apt sum up of the lives of these two great men.

Khawaja Khurshid Anwar, the melodist from Lahore

Khwaja Khurshid Anwar, among the many talented music creators from Lahore, stands out for his originality and innovation. Unlike the West, where music composers form an individual group on their own, in the Indian Subcontinent, the music creator is invariably linked to the film industry. The tunes created are for the specific purpose of being used as songs in movies and therefore are influenced by the situation in the film where the song will be on the screen. For this reason, the music composer, often called the music director, works as a team with the director of the movie, the lyric writer for the song, and the singer who will provide the vocals for the song.

Khwaja Sahib was born in Mianwali in 1912, which means he was in the same age group as Faiz Ahmed Faiz and Sadat Hasan Manto. His maternal grandfather was the Civil Surgeon in Mianwali, and one of his mother's sisters was the first wife of Allama Iqbal.

As the son of a successful advocate from Lahore, he had a comfortable life and was interested in music, poetry, and theatre from his teenage years. Some of the poems he wrote while still in school were published in respected literary magazines in Lahore.

In 1935, he passed the exam for Masters in Philosophy from Government College Lahore, becoming the first person in 30 years to get the First Division and winning the Gold Medal. At his father's insistence, he then appeared in the exam for the Indian Civil Service, and although he did very well in his written exams, the examiners made sure he did not pass by giving him low scores in the oral exams. The reason was the British Government's dislike of him due to Khwaja Sahib's past activities; I will come back to this shortly.

Thus, Khawaja Sahib decided to devote his life to music. He had studied classical music under the mentorship of Ustad Tawakkul Hussain Khan and performed classical music on All India Radio's Lahore station. Subsequently, he became a music composer and after working initially at Delhi Radio, arrived in Bombay around 1940 to become a highly respected film music composer before moving to Pakistan post-partition and continuing his career.

Khawaja Sahib was known to tap on a matchbox when composing his tunes. Once he had a draft tune, he would ask the sarangi master Ustad Nazim Ali Khan to come over and memorize the tune (among the musical instruments, the tonal quality of sarangi is the closest to the human voice). After that, other musicians would join in to develop the tune till it was to Khwaja Sahib's satisfaction. Only then would rehearsal with the vocalist start, which would continue for many days before moving on to the studio to record the song. Many artists did not like such a protracted process of producing a song, but Khwaja Sahib was a perfectionist who believed in quality over quantity. As a result, in his 43-year-long career, Khwaja Sahib created music for only 28 films (10 in India and 18 in Pakistan)!

Among the artists who developed a close working relationship with Khawaja Sahib were the film director Masood Pervaiz, the lyric writers/poets Qateel Shafai and Tanvir Naqvi (who was Madam Noor Jehan's brother-in-law), and the singer Madam Noor Jehan. She later remembered that to sing some of his songs to the standard that he wanted, she sometimes had to practice for months.

His music is suffused with melancholy and longing. In his personal life, he was known to be shy and reclusive. When specifically asked for the reason for the sadness in his music and for his quiet persona, he attributed this to a teenage love for a girl who died when he was not yet 20 years old. This looks like a similar story to Faiz Sahib's becoming a poet, which he attributes to his falling in love with a girl who lived next door to him and was married off when he went to Lahore for his studies.

It's indeed thought that there were other traumatic experiences that shaped Khawaja Sahib's life and music. While still a student in Government College, Khwaja Sahib attended the court hearings of Bhagat Singh's trial. This brought him to the attention of British authorities who looked at every Indian attending this trial with suspicion. The authorities then laid out a trap by using another student who recruited Khwaja Sahib for revolutionary activities. Khwaja Sahib was then arrested and as was standard practice, pressured to become a British informer or to give evidence against other revolutionaries. As he refused all the pressure, he was given a 2-year sentence and spent around 4 months in prison. Later on, some ill-wishers created the rumour that Khwaja Sahib had given evidence against Bhagat Singh. There is no possibility of this being true as Khawaja Sahib did not personally know Bhagat

Singh, but the slander would have hurt him, creating resentment which looks to have lasted a lifetime.

While there is no doubt that Khwaja Sahib would have been against the British Colonial yoke around the neck of India, it would not be fair to paint him purely as an anti-colonialist. It is a tragedy of our times that people are categorized into boxed groups, so they are marked off as anti-colonialist or Marxist, Fundamentalist, etc. While some do fall into these specified categories, others like Khawaja Khurshid Anwar, Bhagat Singh, Sadat Hasan Manto, Sahir Ludhianvi, etc., cannot be arranged in such restrictive boxes. While all of these were against the exploitation of humans by the wealthy, they were not Marxists. No doubt all of them wanted India to be free of British rule, but to them, that was not to be the be-all and end-all of the problems. What they really wanted was a new social order that can only be created by changing the prevalent social and economic hierarchy. Without this fundamental change, the result of the White Imperialists leaving was, as we saw it happen, their replacement by the Brown Imperialists.

The personal bond between Khwaja Sahib and Faiz Sahib, highlights the depth of their relationship and the profound impact they had on each other's lives. It's touching to see how their connection endured until the very end, with Khwaja Sahib's parting words to Faiz Sahib. This was when Faiz went to visit Khwaja Sahib a few days before he passed away and when asked how is he feeling Khwaja Sahib replied in Punjabi, 'Fajay (Faiz's pet name), I am going and will wait for you on the other side.' The day he died a distressed Faiz Sahib lamented that today the last person who called be Faja has departed, Faiz Sahib himself died less than 3 weeks after that.

Khawaja Sahib's legacy extends beyond his individual

compositions; his preservation of classical Indian music in "Ahang-e-Khusravi" is indeed a monumental contribution. By documenting 90 raags rendered by leading musicians of the subcontinent, he ensured that this rich heritage would be passed down to future generations. It's a testament to his dedication to both preserving and innovating within the realm of music.

Khwaja Sahib's work, particularly through songs like those from "Koel" and "Heer Ranjha," underscores the lasting impact of his artistry on audiences. Each listener may have their own cherished memories associated with his music, reflecting the universality and timelessness of his compositions.

Kipling's Lahore

Argentinian writer Jorge Luis Borges (1899-1986) is a towering figure in Spanish literature. From the 20th-century writers, only fellow South American Pablo Neruda can be considered at par with him. Borges's forte was short stories. Due to a familial disease, he started losing his eyesight during his 30s and became completely blind by the time he was in his fifties. Perhaps because of this, his stories are rich in the atmosphere of the inner world, exploring dreams, riddles, and mythology. As a child and teenager, Borges had the chance to travel widely and live in different countries; however, there is no evidence he ever visited Lahore or India. Still, one of his famous stories called 'The Blue Tiger' is set in British colonial India. The central character, who is from Scotland, is a professor at the University in Lahore.

The story moves around within India but ends at the Wazir Khan Mosque in Lahore where the hero in great mental torment finds a cure for his anguish as he realizes the reality of truth,

'I did not sleep the night of 10 February. After a walk that led me far into the dawn, I

passed through the gates of the mosque of Wazir Khan.

It was the hour at which
light has not yet revealed the colours of things. There was not a soul in the
courtyard. Not knowing why, I plunged my hands into the water of the fountain of
ablutions. Inside the mosque, it occurred to me that God and Allah are two names
for a single, inconceivable Being, and I prayed aloud that I be freed from my burden.
Unmoving, I awaited some reply.'

Borges's knowledge about Lahore and Wazir Khan Mosque had come from the writings of British writer Rudyard Kipling (1865-1936), who was born in Bombay and spent his formative years in Lahore. In 1907, Kipling became the first writer in English to be awarded The Nobel Prize in Literature; at 42, he was also the youngest till then. Kipling's novel Kim starts in Lahore, where the young protagonist is sitting astride the Zamzama gun still in place in front of the Museum. However, it looks as if his short story 'The City of Dreadful Night' acted as the inspiration for Borges when he wrote The Blue Tiger. This story takes the readers on a walking tour of old Lahore during a stifling hot summer night, eventually ending at the Wazir Khan Mosque where the narrator climbs one of the minarets of the Mosque before heading home as the night ends.

Kipling's parents belonged to the cadre of British officials and scholars who served in India. Though he spent the first few years of his life in Bombay, he was shipped off to England for education at the age of 5. When he returned, a few months before his 17th birthday, his father John Lockwood Kipling had become the first principal of the Mayo School of Arts in Lahore (now called the National College of Arts and the premier school of arts in Pakistan) as well as the first curator of the Lahore Museum.

Kipling Junior spent just over 5 years in Lahore. As the assistant editor of the Civil and Military Gazette (not that fancy a post when you consider that the only other staff was the editor), Kipling had extensive exposure to the gossip and happenings in Lahore of that time. A lot of the information for his news and stories was sourced to men he met at the Punjab Club, which was his frequent abode. But in addition, he looks to have interacted with the native population, at least by observing them during his frequent nocturnal walks all around the walled old city of Lahore. In this, he was rather unique, as the British residents of Lahore stayed in the Civil Line and Model Town areas, avoiding the walled city like the plague. This was literal, as it was the fear of disease that kept them away.

The Wazir Khan Mosque looks like one of his favourite destinations, perhaps partly because it was a favourite of his father who highly recommended his students to spend time there as it had some of the most original fresco art in the world, although Rudyard does not appear to be much interested in this art. Kipling writes about his Lahore years in some detail in his long article under the title Seven Hard Years. However, he does not provide any description of the various landmarks or the city. For example, he mentions Wazir Khan Mosque in the context of the communal riots that took place in the shadow of the Mosque.

Despite his desire to do so, Kipling was often unable to escape to Simla during the scorching summer months like the rest of his family. He describes the period from mid-April to mid-October alone in the big house, unable to sleep, and spending the time wandering in the streets of Lahore until dawn, visiting strange places like opium dens, watching street dances, or just wandering and looking. No doubt this experience helped him to write his stories and selection of characters for them.

He also tells us the culture of bribery and petty theft was as prevalent in Lahore (and India) then as now. For example, his servant, whenever he went shopping, would deduct a small commission for himself and adjusted for this by inflating the bill he presented to his master. After a little more than 5 years in Lahore, Kipling was posted to Allahabad, which was somewhat of a promotion, but it looks like he did not like it there as much as Lahore. Just over a year later, he decided to leave a salaried job and try becoming a full-time writer; the rest, as they say, is history.

Kipling's most famous novel Kim starts in Lahore with the hero, a 13-year-old British orphan boy perched on the Zamzama gun, which is still present in front of the museum. With him are his two friends, one a high-caste Hindu and the other a poor Muslim; all three are comfortable playing with each other, providing another example of the open, tolerant, and cosmopolitan nature of Lahore in those days.

Javeed Manzil

This is the house where Allama Iqbal spent his last 3 years and is now a museum where many original manuscripts, artifacts, and personal items belonging to Iqbal have been preserved. Our family has a personal connection with the house as well. The construction of the house was supervised by Iqbal's elder brother Sheikh Ata Mohammed, who was a retired civil engineer. Sheikh Ata was the great-grandfather of my mother.

Contrary to the lies propagated by the anti-Iqbal group, Iqbal was never paid a penny by the British Government throughout his life. His studies abroad were mostly financed by his elder brother, and on return, he practiced law at Lahore Chambers. He was not as successful in his law practice as M.A. Jinnah but did better than M.K. Gandhi and P.J. Nehru. Money in the Iqbal household was always tight, and his wife, Sardar Begum, regularly scolded him for wasting his time thinking for hours or writing poetry instead of going to the chambers and finding clients.

The money for the purchase of the land and building the house was mostly from what Sardar Begum had managed to squirrel away over the years and from the sale of her jewellery. Only in the last few years of his life, when due to ill health he could not practice at all, did Iqbal accept a stipend of Rs 500 per month from the Nawab of Bhopal. Here, also, he had refused the offer of a monthly payment for doing nothing, and the Nawab had therefore commissioned him to write a book on the Quran, which would be dedicated to the Nawab and would clearly acknowledge that it was completed with the help of the Nawab (a proof of this in the form of a letter by Sir Ras Masood, who was Iqbal's close friend and the PM of Bahawalpur state, is preserved at this museum).

In addition to family ties, my maternal grandfather was a great scholar of Iqbal who is universally acknowledged to have introduced Iqbal to Iranians in such a way that Iqbal is the only non-Iranian poet of Persian that Iranians acknowledge as a poet of Persian. How Ghalib would have loved to have my grandfather, A.H. Irfani, as his advocate.

Among the items on display, there is a painting that shows Iqbal and his mentor, Maulana Rumi, in the company of Halaj, Ghalib, and Quratul Ain Tahira. Inspired by the poetry of Iqbal, the painting shows those who had a deep impact on him. As we know, both Halaj and Tahira were crucified when they were declared to be heretics. In a world where the majority of heroes and martyrs are men, Iqbal, by including Tahira, whom he named Khaton a Ajam (The Lady from Iran), debunks the claims of those who call Iqbal a misogynist or a religious bigot (besides being a woman, Tahira was from the Bhai sect who are considered non-Muslim like the Ahmadis).

In the verse that accompanies the above painting, Iqbal tells us why the three are to be admired, as it roughly translates as:

'Ghalib, Halaj and Lady of Iran

Created a turmoil in the tranquil world of Islam'.

This aptly sums up Iqbal's philosophy of Islam. It is not that of a dead conformist religion where the followers do what they are told is true, but an active, revolutionary, syncretic religion whose followers challenge the established dogmas and are prepared to die for this.

There are many such ideas ascribed to Iqbal based on the wrong interpretation of his selective poetry. We need to rescue Iqbal from those who have turned him into a jingoistic Islamist and revive him as the true poet of revolution he really is. An Iqbal who is judged not based on a few misplaced out-of-context verses, but in light of the vast corpus of his work analysed and interpreted in the light of the prevailing social and geopolitical situation of the world in those times. This is something not only of academic and historical importance, but an Iqbal resurrected in this way can be the prophet of a true renaissance within Islamic and Eastern society, bringing peace and prosperity to the millions who suffer humiliation, persecution, and hopelessness. Iqbal may be many things, but by far above all he is a poet of change, and change is what we most need at the moment.

Epilogue

'Jo tar say nikli hai woh dhun sub nein suni hai
Jo saz pay guzri hai woh kis dil ko pata hai
Everyone loves the beauty of a heart touching tune
What the creator has to endure for it no one knows'

— *Sahir Ludihanvi*

It is a beautiful spring evening in Lahore as I write these lines to complete my draft so that I can send it to the publisher. For this trip, I arrived in Lahore just over 2 weeks ago, and since then Lahore has been dry, cold, and often foggy, not what I wanted to experience. However, recently we had rain, and the weather has become warm and pleasant. Next week, we have the national elections followed by several cultural and literary festivals. Now that I am getting ready to publish this book, I am still not sure if this is the right thing to do. Today I visited the international book fair, and one can see that there are thousands of books being published on every subject, so I cannot help but wonder what will be served by publishing another. However, my publisher, Mohammad Fahad of AKS

Publishing House, whose family has been settled in Lahore for 500 years and who has a real passion to publish books, has managed to convince me to publish this book.

At times the atmosphere in Lahore, which reflects the rest of Pakistan, feels like the calm before the storm. At the same time, one gets the feeling that no one really cares as everyone has the problems of daily living. Everywhere one goes, there are people and more people, as the city looks overpopulated and teeming with people. The old Lahoris I meet all lament the change the city has undergone over the years, becoming more and more intolerant and religious.

All we can do is hope for a better and brighter future where the old Lahore will return, a Lahore that was renowned for its academic institutions, its intellectuals, its hospitality, and its tolerance.

If you have read this book or even a few articles, I hope that you have enjoyed my ramblings.

Lahore, 4th February 2024.

Printed in Great Britain
by Amazon